CONSPIRACY

Also by P. O'Connell Pearson

Fly Girls
Fighting for the Forest

CONSPIRACY

NiXON, WATERGATE, AND DEMOCRACY'S DEFENDERS

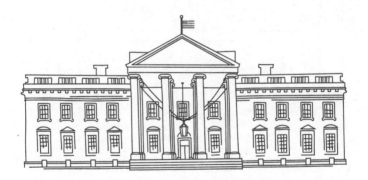

P. O'Connell Pearson

Simon & Schuster Books for Young Readers
NEW YORK   LONDON   TORONTO   SYDNEY   NEW DELHI

SIMON & SCHUSTER BOOKS FOR YOUNG READERS
An imprint of Simon & Schuster Children's Publishing Division
1230 Avenue of the Americas, New York, New York 10020

For my children
Kevin, Michael, Megan, and Kathlin,
the kind of people
that make the future promising

ACKNOWLEDGMENTS

Watergate was a familiar story to me before I started this book. Or so I thought. Diving into the details gave me new insight into the public servants who worked tirelessly to uphold the rule of law and defend the Constitution, and to the journalists and publishers who pursued the truth in a difficult time. I am grateful for their efforts and for their memoirs, histories, recorded interviews, and more. Their reflections and analyses are fascinating as well as informative.

My gratitude to my editor, Liz Kossnar, who suggested that I write about Watergate and had confidence that I would find a way to explain such a complex story to young readers. My thanks also to Kendra Levin and the copy editors, designers, and others at Simon & Schuster Books for Young Readers who did so much to see the project through despite the challenges posed by the 2020 pandemic.

I also thank Joseph Esposito, who shared his expertise and time. And I will always appreciate the wonderful people at Lesley University's MFA program, especially Susan E. Goodman and Chris Lynch, who helped set me on this path.

Thanks as well to my dear friends, writing pals, and family members for their interest, support, and willingness to listen to me go on and on and on. My love and gratitude to my children, children-in-law, and grandchildren for being cheerleaders and all-around wonderful people. And to my husband, Paul, forever.

CONTENTS

CHAPTER 1

Landslide

NOVEMBER 7, 1972

pproval. Richard Nixon had spent his entire life working for approval. Now, as the earliest vote counts came in on election night, 1972, it became clear that he'd finally gotten what he wanted. Not simply a second term as president. No. Nixon had won his first term as president in 1968 with a tiny majority and decided right then that when he ran for a second term, he'd win big, no matter what. He wanted real recognition. He wanted to be an unquestioned, undeniable, undoubted winner. And he'd done it. Richard Milhous Nixon had won a majority of votes in forty-nine of the fifty states. Nixon, a Republican, had defeated his Democratic opponent by nearly eighteen million votes in one of the most lopsided wins in presidential history.

Naturally, Nixon was pleased with the results. Voters had finally recognized his worth. As he saw it, he now had a *mandate*, a kind of authority to act boldly, and he planned to use it. But while Republicans around the

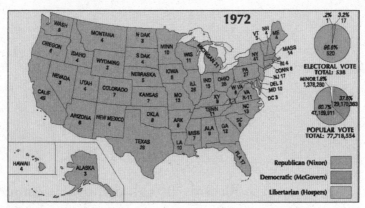

Electoral College totals by state, 1972 presidential election

country cheered the victory, Nixon made just one quick visit to a nearby celebration and a short television appearance to thank his supporters. Then he huddled with two close aides in a room on the second floor of the White House. They talked long into the night, the president serious and unsmiling.

Nixon wrote later that he didn't really know why he was in such a gloomy mood that night. But he thought perhaps he was worried about Vietnam, or perhaps about the upcoming trial in the scandal everyone was calling *Watergate*.[1]

Worry about the war in Vietnam made sense. Nixon had campaigned for his first term in 1968 on a "secret plan" to end the long, long war. He'd reduced the number of

Americans fighting there, but the war still wasn't over and it grew more unpopular by the minute. Nixon believed that the presidents who led the country into the war had made a real mess of things, a mess he was stuck trying to clean up. And it got in the way of everything else he wanted to do as president. In 1972, he campaigned again on ending the war. The situation was complicated, but Nixon was determined to finally achieve peace.

Watergate was another matter. In June, five months before the election, police had interrupted a middle-of-the-night break-in at the Watergate office and apartment complex a mile west of the White House. They arrested the burglars on the spot and soon discovered that the men were somehow connected to Nixon's reelection committee. The story hit the newspapers the next morning, and it could have been very awkward for the president if people believed his campaign staff had done something illegal to try to win votes. But Nixon's press secretary—the White House aide who talks to reporters—went on television and described the crime as a "third-rate burglary" that had nothing to do with the president or any of his aides. Most news outlets soon moved on to other stories, and the burglary faded into the background.

The burglars faced charges related to the break-in and would probably be in the headlines again when they went to trial. But the judge on the case scheduled the trial for *after* the election, and that was good for Nixon. It meant that the story wasn't in the news on Election Day. And by the time it was, most people wouldn't even remember something that had happened in June. Even so, the night before the election, with all the polls predicting a landslide, Nixon wrote in his diary, "The only sour note of the whole thing is Watergate. . . ."[2] Why would that be?

Richard Nixon had worked toward winning the 1972 election by a big margin since the day of the 1968 election. But halfway through his first term as president, he had feared he might not win a second term at all. In 1970, prices for food and housing and gasoline were high and getting higher, and that hurt the president's popularity. People wanted him to fix the economy, and he wanted that too. But he hadn't had much success. At the same time, tens of thousands of college students were shutting down campuses and highways across the country to protest the war in Vietnam and Nixon's war policies. That made many voters angry and afraid and made the president look weak. When the Democrats started their campaign for the 1972 election, they would go after the president on all of it.

At that point, even though the election was two years away, Nixon told his aides to do whatever it took to win

President Nixon greets students in Utica, Michigan, 1972

big in 1972. They followed his order, even using tactics the public could not know about. Tactics that a lot of people would call unfair or underhanded, even criminal. In fact, Nixon's men knew that if Americans found out about everything the president's campaign did, they might say President Nixon *stole* the 1972 election. But Richard Nixon and his aides went ahead with the underhanded tactics because they believed victory was important enough to use any means necessary to achieve it.

For two years, the president's men, as people called his aides (yes, they were all men), got away with dirty tricks, bribes, lies, and more in their effort to guarantee Nixon's win. The botched break-in at the Watergate complex was their only slip, and it really wasn't that terrible a crime. Nixon's press secretary was right—it was a "third-rate burglary." But he was wrong that it had nothing to do with the president or his aides. The problem with Watergate was that if anyone dug too deeply into it, they could uncover enough dirt to destroy *everything*.

As Republican celebrations ended late on election night, Nixon still sat with his aides. At two o'clock in the morning, the president ordered scrambled eggs and bacon from the White House kitchen, and the men continued talking about Nixon's victory and his second term. He and his men believed that he, Richard Nixon, and *only* Richard Nixon, could achieve peace around the world. Nixon had campaigned this time on his vision for world peace and the progress he'd made with China and the Soviet Union, as well as the real chance for an end to the war in Vietnam. He'd also promised better pay for the military, and he'd reminded voters of his first-term achievements—new environmental laws and agencies, reforms in law enforcement, new civil rights programs, and more. He'd even talked about plans for simplifying and smoothing out the workings of the gigantic federal government, something almost everyone agreed the government needed. Those

Richard Nixon (right), and vice-presidential nominee Spiro Agnew at the 1972 Republican National Convention

kinds of promises—his *platform*—as well as a very weak Democratic candidate gave Nixon his huge win.

But Richard Nixon had other second-term plans on his mind that night too. Plans that weren't in his public platform. Unofficial plans that, like the secret campaign tactics, no one could know about. Plans that would shock the people who had just voted for him.

• • •

Americans thought they knew Richard Nixon well in November 1972. They knew he grew up poor in California with a cold, stern father and not enough money. He had worked at his father's store, helped care for his younger brothers, and still earned excellent grades. He was smart and studious, willing to work harder than anyone else, and he'd learned at a very young age not to give up. No matter what. Not when a younger brother died at the age of seven, and not when his older brother died eight years later after a long battle with tuberculosis. Even when he got into Harvard but couldn't afford to go, Richard Nixon refused to give up. He went to a nearby college, where he again worked harder than anyone else, and then went on to law school. Americans admired that kind of personal story. Many liked Nixon's grit and his willingness to press on against the odds.

That life story and some tough campaigning won Richard Nixon his first election in 1946 when he ran for the House of Representatives from a district in Southern California. Four years later, he won election to the Senate. In 1952, he was elected vice president under Dwight Eisenhower, and they won reelection together in 1956. But when Nixon ran for president in 1960 against Democrat John F. Kennedy, he lost by one-tenth of one percent in the closest race in US history. That hurt, and after losing the race for governor of California in 1962, Nixon thought about getting out of politics. But he wasn't a quitter. He spent time studying his mistakes, learning about voters in every part of the country, and thinking about new ways for the United States to work with foreign countries. In 1968, he ran for president again and got just enough votes to win.

The trouble was that while people recognized Nixon as intelligent, hardworking, and determined, that was only one side of the man. Even his closest aides and advisors eventually admitted that he had a very dark side as well.

For example, instead of thinking of political opponents as men and women who disagreed with him on the issues, Richard Nixon thought of them as enemies. To him, that meant that bending or breaking the rules to defeat them was all right. From the very start of his political career he'd lied about the people he ran against, saying they were communists. By 1972, he didn't want to defeat Democrats—he wanted to destroy them.

Nixon also thought journalists and reporters who criticized his speeches or actions were out to get him. He believed that they treated him unfairly and favored other politicians. It didn't stop there. College professors who disagreed with his views of history or economics? Enemies. Celebrities, business executives, civil rights leaders, war protesters who spoke out against his policies? All enemies. Especially the war protesters.

Nixon saw so many people and groups as enemies that during his first term as president, his aides created an "enemies list" with the names of individuals, groups, organizations, even colleges and universities he believed wanted to ruin him. Eventually, the list—kept locked in a safe—grew to hundreds of names.

Between his first election in 1968 and his reelection four years later, Nixon's determination to win big had made his dark side stronger. He was sincere about seeking world peace and improving military pay as he said he would. But he didn't plan to use his victory to unite the country the way many presidents try to do. Instead, his secretary of state, Henry Kissinger, said later,

> It was as if victory was not an occasion for reconciliation [setting aside differences] but an opportunity to settle the scores of a lifetime.[3]

The enemies list had started as a "don't invite these people to the White House" list. Now it became a list of people and groups Nixon wanted to demolish during his second term. A month before the 1972 election he told a White House lawyer,

All of those that have tried to do us in . . . are asking for it and they are going to get it. We haven't used the Bureau [FBI] and we haven't used the Justice Department, but things are going to change.[4]

When Nixon said he would *use* those government departments, he meant that he would order the FBI—Federal Bureau of Investigation—to investigate his enemies, to tap their phones, look at their mail, and perhaps talk to their employers. He'd done it a year earlier when a reporter for CBS News told television viewers that something Nixon said in a speech wasn't true. The reporter was correct, but Nixon was furious and within forty-eight hours, FBI agents arrived at the reporter's house and office while other agents visited his family, friends, and coworkers to do a "background check."[5] Why? The agents may have thought the president was considering the reporter for a job, but in fact, he simply wanted to inconvenience and bully the man.

Nixon planned to use the Internal Revenue Service—the agency that collects Americans' taxes—the same way. Even if IRS agents didn't find anything wrong in someone's tax filings, they could bother a person for all sorts of financial records going back years and ask detailed questions about everything they'd earned or spent. The agents didn't need to know why they were investigating— the president could call it national security or a background check. Even if the truth was that he was just after his Democratic opponents. He told aides, "We ought to persecute them" using the IRS.[6] Persecute? Yes, by forcing innocent people to spend lots of money on lawyers and accountants, and lots of time—months or even years— worrying they'd done something wrong when they hadn't.

Nixon and his men had other ideas to take out his enemies as well. White House aides could give or *leak* embarrassing or damaging information on an enemy to reporters. The president had tried it in 1971. At the time, he wanted to get hold of negative information about his predecessor, Democratic president Lyndon Johnson, and decisions Johnson had made on the war in Vietnam. If he could leak that information to the press, it would be a huge embarrassment to Johnson and to the Democrats still in Congress. An aide told Nixon that the documents were in a safe at a private research organization in Washington. Nixon told his men to ". . . get in and get those files. Blow the safe and get it."[7] The burglary and safe-blowing never happened, and it turned out that the documents Nixon thought would be so damaging didn't exist. Not in that safe or anywhere else.

Wait. What about the US Constitution and the law?

First, Richard Nixon was the president of the United States. He made the same promise all presidents make. It's spelled out in Article II of the US Constitution: "I do solemnly swear (or affirm) that I will faithfully execute [carry out] the Office of President of the United States, and will to the best of my Ability, preserve, protect and defend the Constitution of the United States." As the head of the executive branch of government, it is the president's job to make sure agencies enforce the nation's laws and follow the Constitution. Think about that.

Second, the first ten amendments to the Constitution are called the Bill of Rights. The First Amendment guarantees freedom of speech and freedom of the press. Reporters, newspapers, and other news media may freely and openly criticize the government, including the president. So can private individuals. And the Fourth Amendment guarantees that citizens will be safe from government or police searches unless a judge agrees there is serious reason for them.

Breaking and entering, stealing documents, blowing up a safe? All illegal—they are crimes. So is wiretapping phones without a judge's okay. That's the Fourth Amendment again.

President Nixon didn't plan to break into any offices or listen in on reporters' phone calls himself. But legally, ordering a criminal action is just as bad as committing the actual crime.

The American people didn't know about the president's secret plans when they voted, of course. They had no idea what was going on behind the closed doors of the White House or what kinds of actions Nixon had ordered.

Hardly anyone did. But the president's friend and former attorney general John Mitchell later called these secrets the "White House horrors."[8]

The horrors went beyond attacks on "enemies." They included taking bribes from businesses that wanted government favors and accepting illegal campaign donations. They even included sabotaging the election.

Nixon's men knew that the president wanted to run against someone he was certain to defeat. So they came up with a plan for a secret "dirty tricks" campaign.

Senator Edmund Muskie of Maine was the Democrats' most popular candidate in early 1972. But his campaign began to fall apart before the Democratic Convention. Ads for Muskie rallies listed wrong times or dates. Workers arrived late. A newspaper printed a letter showing that Muskie used offensive and insulting language. The same paper printed accusations of racism and heavy drinking by Muskie's wife. Muskie and his supporters didn't know what was happening. No matter what they did, the campaign was a mess. Other Democratic candidates had similar experiences. George McGovern, unlikely to do well in the November election, ended up winning the Democratic nomination.

All of it was part of Nixon's order to his aides that anything and everything was acceptable to make sure he won.

Wait. Can they do that?

Much of what Nixon's people did was not strictly illegal. But that didn't make it right. It was *unethical* at the very least. That means that their actions— their "dirty tricks"—went against accepted values or ideas of right and wrong. They weren't playing fair. And they were also going against one of the most important principles of representative democracy— free and fair elections. Without fair elections, there is no democracy.

There was even more to Nixon's secret plans than getting back at his opponents or winning the election at all costs. His ideas for reorganizing the government went well beyond what he had said in public, too. Richard Nixon wanted to make decisions and appointments and run the government without asking Congress for approval. He didn't want the House of Representatives or the Senate to block his plans or tell him how to spend money or who he could appoint to high offices. That wasn't unusual; most modern presidents have wanted more authority. Over the years, the federal government had become so enormous and slow-moving that presidents had difficulty carrying out their plans and fulfilling their campaign promises. But

Nixon's ideas went beyond what earlier presidents had considered.

For example, Nixon had decided that while Congress had the job of *appropriating* or approving money for specific uses, he would *impound* or refuse to spend the money when he disagreed with Congress. He also had decided to reduce Congress's influence on how he ran executive departments and policies. In the American system of government, the president *appoints* cabinet members—heads of major departments like the Department of the Interior and the Department of Agriculture and so on—but the Senate must *confirm* or approve those appointments. Nixon wanted to get around that check on his authority. He would appoint cabinet officers who the Senate would confirm easily. Then he'd have a small group of trusted advisors who did not need Senate approval make the big decisions and tell the department heads what to do. Later, the press called these advisors "super-secretaries." Nixon had planned to establish this new structure without asking Congress for a reorganization law as earlier presidents had. But was that constitutional?

In addition to shrinking Congress's role in spending decisions and appointments, Nixon planned to "clean house" of anyone anywhere in the White House who wasn't loyal to Richard Nixon first and foremost. And he wanted the same kind of loyalty from the people who worked in all of the executive agencies of the federal government. These people are called *civil servants* and often spend their entire careers in government service. They stay in their jobs no matter who the president is or what party he or she belongs to. The president doesn't appoint them. They earn their positions through education, expertise, and hard work.

Nixon couldn't check on the loyalty of each and every civil servant—there were over two million nonmilitary workers in government buildings in Washington and around the country (about the same number as there are today). But those with real authority had better make their loyalty to the president clear if they wanted to keep their jobs. They needed to jump when Nixon's men said "jump" no matter what their expertise and experience told them. Nixon didn't want their input or questions about issues or investigations or anything else. He wanted total obedience and loyalty in order to have a government in which he, the president, had complete control.

Just a second.
What would the framers think of all this?

The framers or writers of the United States Constitution—James Madison, George Washington,

Roger Sherman, James Wilson, and more than fifty other men who came together and designed a new government in 1787—were determined that no one person would ever have total control in the new country. They'd fought a long, bloody war to break away from a king and they weren't going to go back. Madison had studied every kind of government from the ancient Greeks through the eighteenth century and brought his ideas to the Constitutional Convention. After great debate and compromise, the delegates decided on a representative democracy or republic with three equal branches of government. The president, head of the executive branch, carries out the law but does not have more power than the legislative branch (Congress, made up of the House of Representatives and the Senate), which writes the law. And neither the president nor the Congress has more power than the judicial branch (the federal courts with the Supreme Court at the top), which determines what the law means. This idea is called *separation of powers*. Additionally, each branch of government has ways to oversee or check the power of the other two. That's the *system of checks and balances*. The framers knew that a government with a stronger executive could be more efficient and fast-moving than the government they designed. A powerful king, for example, could make decisions very quickly because he didn't have to ask for approval from anyone. It was the framers' belief, however, that those governments didn't guard citizens' rights or uphold democratic ideals. Any single person or group with total control was dangerous, no matter who that person or group was. But Richard Nixon wanted to make the president or executive much more powerful than Congress or the courts. And he wanted to shrink the other branches' ability to check executive power.

The framers also understood that presidents would naturally want aides and advisors who are loyal to them. But loyalty to one person above anything else? No. That would make that one person more important than the Constitution. Look at the oath all government employees take: "I do solemnly swear (or affirm) that I will support and defend the Constitution of the United States against all enemies, foreign and domestic [inside the country]; that I will bear true faith and allegiance to the same [the Constitution]; that I take this obligation freely, without any mental reservation or purpose of evasion; and that I will well and faithfully discharge the duties of the office on which I am about to enter." Think about where every government worker promises to put his or her highest loyalty.

Nixon hadn't accomplished all that he wanted to during his first term. He blamed his enemies, many of them in Congress and the news media. But now he saw a chance to move forward without checks and really get things done. Imagine that.

Imagine a president of the United States without any checks from Congress. Imagine a news media that is afraid to criticize that president or let the public know about government corruption or lies that may affect people's jobs, their families, or the nation. Imagine elections where only one candidate has any real chance of winning. What else would that president or a future president do? Imagine the Constitution with no meaning and a Bill of Rights that protects no rights at all.

Richard Nixon wanted to be a great president. By 1972, however, his dark side became too strong. Most Americans didn't know it yet, but the president they had just reelected—and the men he chose as his closest advisors and aides—were a real danger to American democracy.

* * *

On election night, the president's men thought Nixon was safe. They'd handled that one slip—Watergate—by giving the arrested men a lot of money to either stay silent or tell lies in court. Now that the election was over, they'd keep paying the burglars if they had to, and make sure the prosecutors at the trial didn't dig up any information that would be harmful to the president.

The president's men were wrong. They and the president were not safe. The framers had designed a system of government that could survive a president who put himself above the presidential oath, above the Constitution, and above the law. The system would work—*if* enough people *made* it work.

Even as Richard Nixon talked to his aides and ate his scrambled eggs on election night, the constitutional system was in motion. The system had been in motion since the night of the Watergate break-in in June. That system was chugging forward like a slow but powerful locomotive.

CHAPTER 2

A Bungled Break-in
JUNE 17, 1972

At nine o'clock on a warm Saturday morning five months before the 1972 election, Bob Woodward's phone rang. His editor at the *Washington Post*'s local news desk needed him in the office—there'd been a burglary and he wanted Woodward to cover it.

Woodward, a graduate of Yale University, had spent five years as an officer in the navy and planned to go to Harvard Law School. But he decided to go into journalism instead. He managed to land a job at the *Washington Post* after just a year with a local Maryland paper. His editors told him to work on his writing, but they liked that he was smart and energetic, and knew how to get to the heart of a story.

Woodward didn't mind Saturday assignments eating into his weekend. But after nine months at the *Washington Post*, he'd hoped to be investigating bigger things than burglaries. Oh well, with luck he'd get a meaty assignment, a real investigation, soon.

Bob Woodward hurried to the office, expecting to find things fairly quiet on a Saturday morning. Instead, the place buzzed with news of the burglary at the Democratic Party offices. Police had arrested five men in the middle of the night, all wearing business suits and surgical gloves. They'd been carrying cameras, film, tiny tear-gas guns, telephone bugging equipment, and a lot of cash—over two thousand dollars, most of it in hundred-dollar bills. The city police had called in the FBI, the country's top law enforcement organization.

This was no ordinary burglary, Woodward realized. Not if the FBI was involved. And most burglars breaking into a place plan to steal something. They don't bring cameras and telephone bugs with them. These guys weren't regular thieves—they had to be after information.

Woodward had assumed that the burglars broke into a local Democratic Party office, where volunteers gather to hand out buttons and yard signs and that sort of thing. He was mistaken. The burglary was at the offices of the Democratic National Committee, the headquarters of the entire Democratic Party nationwide. Suddenly, the assignment didn't feel quite so small and local.[9]

Woodward got down everything the *Post*'s nighttime police reporter knew. A young security guard named Frank Wills had worked for just a few months at the

Washington Post investigative reporter Bob Woodward

Watergate—a very posh office, hotel, and apartment complex along the Potomac River in Washington, DC. Wills knew there'd been a couple of attempted break-ins at the offices earlier in the spring, so he was on alert as he made his rounds. Shortly after midnight, as Friday became Saturday, Wills saw a piece of tape covering the automatic lock on a door leading from the garage into the building. He peeled it off so the lock would catch when the door shut and then continued his rounds. This wasn't that unusual. Maintenance workers sometimes taped the locks so they could go in and out easily. People in the upstairs offices did the same thing when they needed to move boxes or equipment, so the tape didn't really worry Wills. He figured that whoever put the tape on the door forgot to remove it. But when he came back past the same door later, he saw a new piece of tape. Alarmed, he called the police.

Two plainclothes officers happened to be nearby and answered the call. They caught five burglars red-handed in a fifth-floor office. The men didn't struggle or resist arrest, and the police took them to jail around three a.m. They would appear before a judge later that same Saturday for a brief hearing. Woodward headed for the courthouse.

He was surprised to see a couple of expensively dressed men sitting in the courtroom when he arrived. Most people arrested for burglary in the middle of the night can't afford their own lawyers, he thought. The court generally appoints one to represent them. But these guys sure looked like lawyers. And based on the quality of their suits and briefcases, Woodward guessed they were pricey lawyers, not the low-paid *public defenders* the court appointed. He tried to ask them why they were there, but they wouldn't talk to him. Still, Woodward felt sure they had some connection to the five suspects or they wouldn't be in the courtroom. But how did a bunch of burglars come up

Jefferson and the Watergate office complex in Washington, DC, with the memorials and the Potomac River in the background.

with expensive lawyers so quickly, especially on a weekend?

A few minutes later, the suspects walked into the courtroom behind a marshal, and Woodward glanced at their rumpled suits. The rumple didn't surprise him—ten or twelve hours in a jail cell will do that. And the night reporter had said the five had on business suits when they were arrested. Seeing their suits now, though, made Woodward wonder why burglars would wear business clothes for a midnight break-in. The whole situation seemed odd.

As soon as the judge opened the hearing, the prosecutor—the government lawyer who presents the evidence against the accused—asked the judge to deny the men the opportunity to *post bond*—pay money to get out of jail while they waited for their trials. He argued that the five suspects should stay in jail until their trial because they had given the police fake names and they didn't have families or jobs nearby. This indicated that they might leave the country before their trial date—which could be months in the future—if the judge set them free. The prosecutor argued that the court should not trust them.

If police catch burglars red-handed, shouldn't the burglars go right to prison?

That would make things simple, but simple isn't always fair or legal. The United States Constitution protects the rights of people accused of a crime, even those who are caught in the act.

Police must tell arrested people why they are being arrested and read them their rights—the right to remain silent, the right to have an attorney, and more. The accused must go to court soon after the arrest, where a judge asks if they understand their rights and the charges against them.

The judge also decides whether the accused can be trusted to return to court for trial. If so, the accused may pay bail or a bond and leave jail. When they appear for trial, they get the bond money back. Since some accused people cannot be trusted to come to court for a trial without some pressure, the money is an incentive. Others who might flee or commit more crimes remain in jail until their trial. Unfortunately, those who can be trusted to return for their trials but cannot afford bail often remain in jail awaiting trial as well, something several states are working to change.

The accused goes to prison only after a trial and after the prosecutor proves to a jury "beyond a reasonable doubt" that the accused person is guilty of the charges.

The judge asked the men if they had jobs. One of them stood to speak for all five as Woodward wrote down everything he could hear. They were "anti-communists," the spokesman said. Woodward paused. Anti-communists? How could being against communism (a set of political and economic beliefs) be a job? The judge told the suspect to come to the bench or desk and explain himself. Woodward wanted to hear this. He moved closer just in time to catch the man whisper his name: James McCord. He was a security consultant and used to work for the government, he told the judge very quietly. What part of the government? McCord paused and Woodward moved even closer, straining to hear what might come next.

Finally, McCord murmured, "The CIA."

"Holy . . . ," Woodward breathed. Had he heard McCord correctly? The look on the judge's face told him he had. The CIA was the Central Intelligence Agency, the nation's top organization for gathering information from around the world to protect national security. There were all sorts of jobs in the CIA, but the one most people knew best was *spy*, what the CIA called an *operative*.

Why would someone who'd been with the CIA break into an American political office in Washington, DC?

Woodward practically ran out of the courthouse, hailed a cab, and raced back to the newsroom. This burglary was strange and getting stranger by the minute. What he'd heard in that courtroom had to make it into Sunday's paper.[10]

The *Post*'s city editor put eight reporters on the break-in story so they could have it ready by six thirty Saturday evening, the deadline for the next morning's paper. As the time drew near, his boss, the managing editor, came into the office and read the final draft of the article. "That's a hell of a story," he said.[11] Woodward had gotten his wish. The local burglary assignment was national news—important national news at that. The first several paragraphs would be on Sunday's front page with the rest of the piece inside the paper.

The next morning when Washingtonians lifted their thick Sunday newspapers from their driveways or front porches, they saw a headline reading, "5 Held in Plot to Bug Democrats' Office Here."

> Five men, one of whom said he is a former employee of the Central Intelligence Agency, were arrested at 2:30 A.M. yesterday in what authorities described as an elaborate plot to bug the offices of the Democratic National Committee here....

The story's first paragraph did what a news article's first paragraph should do—it answered who, what, when, where, and why or how. The next two paragraphs filled in more details. But even with eight reporters working all day to figure the story out, the fourth paragraph said,

> There was no immediate explanation as to why the five suspects would want to bug the Democratic National Committee offices or whether or

not they were working for any other individuals
or organizations.[12]

None of the reporters had been able to identify who
or what was behind the attempted bugging. There wasn't
anything of cash value in that office, so these burglars
weren't planning to walk away from the break-in with
any money or valuables, it seemed. Someone must have
paid them to commit the crime and paid for the bugging
equipment, the tear gas, and the rest. Who? It turned out
that the judge had denied the prosecutor's request that
the men stay in jail. He set bond. And someone paid that
bond within hours. Who did that? And where had those
expensive-looking lawyers come from?

The reporters had far more questions than answers.

A second, shorter story on the break-in also made the
deadline for Sunday's paper. Reporter Carl Bernstein had
pulled together enough information about the burglars to
write several hundred words. Four of the five men lived
in Miami, Florida, he reported, and three were originally
from Cuba. All of them including McCord, the only suspect who lived near Washington, apparently had connections to the CIA. The article appeared on page twenty-one
of the paper's head section with Bernstein's *byline* or name
on it, something Bob Woodward noticed and resented:

Washington Post investigative reporter Carl Bernstein in the *Post* newsroom Washington

Credit for the front-page story went to the *Post*'s police reporter who gave Woodward the arrest details. Woodward and the others were listed at the very end of the article.[13]

At the time of the Watergate break-in in June 1972, Bob Woodward and Carl Bernstein didn't know each other very well at all. Both were just fine with that. They were about the same age—twenty-nine and twenty-eight—and both were serious reporters at the *Post*. But that's where the similarities ended. Unlike newcomer Woodward, Carl Bernstein had been at the paper for six years and before that at the *Post*'s competition, the *Washington Star*. He'd worked his way up from the bottom, starting as a teenage copy boy running errands in the newsroom. Bernstein had gone to college but dropped out before graduating, so there were no Yales or Harvards on his job applications. Yet he wrote very well and very quickly—important skills in the newspaper business.

Woodward didn't like the way Bernstein wormed his way onto stories no one had assigned to him and then got his name on them. Today was just the most recent example. On the other hand, Bernstein figured Woodward had probably leaned on his Ivy League degree rather than really earning his position at the *Washington Post*. And everyone knew Mr. Yale couldn't write worth beans.

Whatever the two thought of each other, though, the city editor had asked them on Saturday night to come back to the office on Sunday and get more answers on the burglary. Both young men wanted to follow up on the break-in story, but they weren't happy about sharing the assignment. They realized, though, that they'd have to work together for at least a while if they were going to get to the bottom of Watergate.[14]

CHAPTER 3

Investigating

JUNE–JULY 1972

T he reporters arrived at the office ready to get to work on Sunday. But they didn't have much to go on. Who might want information on the Democratic National Committee? The obvious answer was the GOP (Grand Old Party, a nickname for the Republican Party), but that would have made a lot more sense a year earlier. In 1971, polls showed that less than half of the country's voters approved of the job Richard Nixon was doing. It looked like he might not win a second term.

Nixon knew his strength as president was in foreign policy and world affairs. In February 1972, he made a very public visit to communist China, part of his strategy to ease tensions and promote peace. No president had ever gone to a communist capital before, but Nixon thought it was time to do things differently. He hoped to open trade between China and the US, and he made some real progress. The public saw the trip as a huge success. It was.

Three months later, in May, the president visited the communist Soviet Union (today's non-communist Russia). Again, his success showed that Richard Nixon was making the world safer. His popularity soared just as the 1972 presidential campaign heated up in the early spring.

At the same time, the Democrats' most likely candidates fell in the polls as Muskie and his challengers saw their campaigns struggle. No one knew at the time that Nixon's people were sabotaging them. In June, less than a week before the Watergate break-in, surveys showed Nixon leading the race 53 percent to 34 percent, nearly unbeatable.[15] It seemed clear to Woodward and Bernstein that Nixon's campaign had no reason to take risks at that point.

Still scratching their heads, Bob Woodward and Carl Bernstein turned to the lists of names they both kept—men and women who always seemed to know what was going on in Washington. Reporters rely on *sources*, people who talk to them privately about what they know. They had names of a few fairly high-level government people, an FBI agent or two, people in the local Metropolitan Police Department. Names of government workers they knew from covering other stories or from college classes or from parties they'd been to. Names of friends' friends and friends' relatives and coworkers. This was years before e-mail or texting. They started calling everyone they could think of who might know something about the burglars, who was who in the Nixon administration or the reelection committee—anything.

Another news organization reported that James McCord—the burglar who admitted he'd worked for the CIA—was the head of security for the Committee to Reelect the President (CRP). CRP wasn't part of the Nixon administration or part of the government in any way. It was an independent group working with the Republican Party and running the president's reelection campaign. Woodward and Bernstein worked to find out more about McCord.

The two reporters learned that McCord owned a security company hired by CRP. They got the address of the business and called all the other businesses located in the same building to find anyone who might know McCord. They also talked to people who had worked with McCord over the years and then to people who lived near him. What kind of man was he? How would anyone describe him? Religious, hardworking, a good father, a coach, responsible. And yet a midnight burglar? The puzzle kept getting more complicated.

By late afternoon the reporters had enough solid facts to write a story for Monday's paper. "GOP Security Aide Among 5 Arrested in Bugging Affair." The headline appeared at the top of the *Post*'s front page, and the article quoted John Mitchell, the president's campaign manager and head of CRP. McCord and the others, Mitchell said, "were not operating on our behalf or with our consent . . . There is no place in our campaign . . . for this type of activity . . ."[16]

Most people paying any attention to the story on Monday morning—Democrats as well as Republicans—accepted Mitchell's statement. Perhaps a few campaign workers got carried away with helping the president, they thought. But they didn't believe the Republican Party was involved with the break-in. That would be absurd. Woodward and Bernstein found it hard to imagine such a thing themselves. But their job was to follow the evidence.

Wait a minute. Washington's police department and the FBI were investigating the break-in. So why were a couple of reporters doing all this digging?

Journalists report the who, what, when, where, and why or how of all sorts of events every day. *Investigative* journalists do more. They dig into the actions of men and women in government and business who may be abusing their positions. They look for illegal or corrupt or money-wasting activity and let the public know when they find it. If a representative democracy such as the United States is to survive, its citizens—the American people—must know what their government is doing, good or bad.

Many presidents and other politicians criticize the media and some have tried to limit its freedom. They'd like to stop journalists from criticizing them. The same is true in other democratic nations. But unlike many non-democratic countries where the news media is an agency of the government just like the Energy Department or Transportation Department, in the US and other representative democracies, television, newspapers, radio, and most social media platforms, are independent organizations and businesses and not controlled by the government.

The US Constitution's First Amendment states, "Congress shall make no law . . . abridging [restricting] the freedom of speech or of the press [publications]."

Thomas Jefferson said in 1786, "Our liberty depends on the freedom of the press . . ."[17] He came to despise newspapers' criticism of him while he was president. But years later, he still believed that "Where the press is free and every man able to read, all is safe."[18]

Very late Sunday night, after the article went to print for Monday's paper, a *Post* reporter who covered police activity called Bob Woodward. Two of the burglars had address books on them when the police arrested them, he said. (Before cell phones, many people carried these tiny notepads with grids for names, addresses, and phone numbers.) The burglars' address books both listed someone named Howard Hunt with "W.H." or "W. House" next to the name. Woodward tried to focus. Who was Howard Hunt? And could "W. House" really mean what he thought it did?

The next day, Monday, Woodward called the White House and asked for Howard Hunt. He expected the operator to tell him no one by that name worked there, but she didn't. It turned out that Hunt worked part-time as a consultant to the president's lawyer or special counsel. Stunned, Woodward called the business where Hunt worked full-time and asked for him. Moments later, Hunt came on the phone. Woodward identified himself and asked if Hunt could explain why his name was in address books belonging to the Watergate burglars. Howard Hunt's surprise and upset came through the phone loud and clear before he slammed down the receiver in Woodward's ear.[19]

Woodward kept digging. He discovered that Hunt had

The address book of one of the men arrested at the Watergate complex. The second entry on the right lists "HH" and two phone numbers, one marked "WH" for White House.

been in the CIA for years and that the FBI considered him a key suspect in the break-in. Woodward started writing an article for Tuesday's paper.[20] Maybe it was possible that the Republican Party was somehow involved in the break-in after all.

So far, the president hadn't commented on Watergate. But on Thursday, two days after the *Washington Post* published

Woodward's article, Nixon told a group of reporters, "The White House has had no involvement whatever in this particular incident."

"No involvement whatever . . ." That was clear enough. But Woodward and Bernstein both noticed the last part of what the president said: ". . . this particular incident." It could be nothing, but with so many strange details popping up, the phrase stood out. ". . . this particular incident." Did that mean there were *other* incidents?

More news came in. The police and the FBI revealed that they suspected two men in addition to the five burglars. The two had coordinated the break-in. And the money the burglars carried came from the Committee to Reelect the President. Bob Woodward and Carl Bernstein kept asking questions.

Sources told Woodward and Bernstein that Nixon's campaign had collected millions of dollars illegally. They'd broken the laws that limited how much money a business or individual could donate and how a campaign had to report donations. The reporters asked themselves how and why a campaign organization would do that. Had CRP promised people or businesses government favors in exchange for donations? That would be soliciting (asking for) bribes. Had someone at the committee threatened to release embarrassing or damaging information if a person didn't make a donation? That would be extortion or black-mail. Why would the Committee to Reelect the President do that kind of thing? Why take the risk of being caught?

Then they learned that some of the Miami men arrested for the June break-in at the Watergate had stayed

Carl Bernstein (left) and Bob Woodward were the only *Washington Post* reporters assigned full time to the Watergate story.

at a Washington hotel for a few days in May. The security people at the Watergate reported burglaries or attempted break-ins at that same time. Could it be just a coincidence?

Only two weeks had passed since the arrests at the Watergate offices, though it felt much longer than that. The *Post* reporters were still scrambling, and the police and FBI were investigating when John Mitchell suddenly resigned as Nixon's campaign manager. Suspicion hung in the air. This story wasn't going to go away.

By late July, Bob Woodward and Carl Bernstein had been investigating the Watergate break-in for six weeks. They'd written story after story, followed leads that worked and leads that turned into dead ends, and still, they didn't know who had planned the break-in or exactly why. Discouraged, Woodward left on a brief vacation and Bernstein started working on other stories. But they weren't happy that Watergate seemed to have dried up. Neither reporter could stop thinking about it. Something was just so fishy and they felt certain they weren't yet near the bottom of it all.

The *New York Times* was one of the few newspapers in the country besides the *Washington Post* still covering the story. It reported that officials in Florida were investigating calls one of the burglars made to CRP in the weeks before the break-in. Bernstein got busy tracking down the

Florida investigators and then flew to Miami on a Monday morning. Woodward, just back in the office, started calling his sources again. Barely an hour before the deadline for the next day's paper, the story came together.

In April, a check for $25,000 appeared in a Miami bank account that belonged to one of the Watergate burglars. But the check wasn't made out to the burglar. It was made out to someone on the finance committee at CRP who insisted that he had given it to CRP's finance chairman. Yet government inspectors couldn't find the check recorded anywhere in the campaign's books even though the law said campaigns had to record every donation. That campaign contribution hadn't paid for advertising or campaign workers' salaries. It had gone straight into the bank account of a man caught breaking into the Watergate offices. Who was responsible?

Woodward wrote furiously as the clock ticked. When he finished, he took the story to his editor, who read it quickly but carefully with his usual pen in hand and a pipe in his mouth. Woodward waited as the editor put down the pen and pipe. He looked at Woodward and said, "We've never had a story like this. Just never."[21]

CHAPTER 4

Worrisome Facts

AUGUST–SEPTEMBER 1972

When other Post reporters started calling them *Woodstein*, Woodward and Bernstein knew they'd gotten over their resentment of each other. On most mornings they met in the office break room, drinking bad vending machine coffee, talking about the story, and sharing their work. If one made suggestions or additions to an article, the other didn't get upset, and they decided to put both their names on every article about Watergate no matter which of them had done the most research or writing.

The two weren't the only reporters investigating Watergate, but they were the only ones assigned to the story full-time. Other *Post* reporters joked about the way they worked and how much time they spent together.

Both Woodward and Bernstein kept track of every conversation they had in person or on the phone and collected hundreds of pages of notes. Woodward used small notepads that fit in his coat pocket, while Bernstein had

Bob Woodward (left) and Carl Bernstein filled several filing cabinets with their notes and made hundreds of phone calls.

a habit of writing on anything handy—notepads, scraps of paper, napkins—as he interviewed people. Neither of them dared to get rid of any of it. Eventually they had over three hundred sources and four entire filing cabinets stuffed with notes and drafts.

But as the days dragged on, fewer and fewer people in the Nixon administration or at CRP would talk to them. One source after another dried up. Getting the kind of information that filled their files grew more difficult.

The two reporters started spending their evenings with lists of names and addresses of people who worked at the White House or for the Committee to Reelect the President, people they hadn't talked to before. They drove around knocking on doors after work and dinner hours when people were likely to be at home. Often, the person they hoped to talk with slammed the door in their faces. It was tedious, frustrating work, but sometimes they had good luck and found someone who was willing to speak to them.

A pattern appeared in what they heard in those nighttime conversations. Several White House and CRP employees had gotten orders to destroy all sorts of records in the days right after the break-in. These were the secretaries, receptionists, bookkeepers, and others who saw documents and screened phone calls every day. But the FBI had never talked to most of them. Never asked questions about documents or phone calls or meetings or anything else.

Many of the men and women who talked to Woodward and Bernstein as the election drew near spoke softly even in their own homes. They seemed nervous, frightened. One told Bernstein to please go "before they see you." Another answered the door and started to cry, saying, "It's all so awful." She wouldn't say anything else.[22] Several worried that their phones were bugged. Others had the feeling they were being watched or followed.[23] And one staffer told them, ". . . don't ever call me on the telephone—God, especially not at work . . . nobody knows what they'll do. They are desperate."[24]

Who were *they*? And what did these people think would happen if they talked? They wouldn't say.

Carl Bernstein had once met a woman who worked at CRP and now he asked her out to lunch. Perhaps she could help him figure things out. She told him right away, "I'm being followed." He thought that sounded awfully dramatic. But she went on, "They know everything at the Committee [to Reelect the President]." *They*. She wouldn't give any names but told Bernstein that the unnamed people knew what was going to happen with the burglary in court. She thought at least three people at CRP knew about the bugging ahead of time. And like the reporters' other sources, she was concerned that the FBI had not asked her any serious questions. "You'll never get the truth," she said. ". . . nobody will ever know what happened."[25]

Both Bernstein and Woodward had felt tense nearly all the time in the last couple of weeks. They'd tried to tell themselves it was just because the people they interviewed were so tense. Bernstein's lunch companion was certainly nervous—it must be contagious. But when she told him that her bosses at CRP knew that he and Woodward had been talking to people at night, it seemed to confirm his vague suspicion that someone was watching him and Bob Woodward.[26]

Were their phones bugged at work or at home? And if someone was following them, who was it? They had no real evidence of anything like that. But as fall came, the two reporters continually felt jumpy as well as tired.

Many of the reporters' sources were people on the edges of the Watergate story. They held fairly low-level positions and had no way of knowing all that went on at the White House or at CRP. But Bob Woodward knew one person who worked high up in the executive branch of government and who actually had direct information from the FBI and CRP and the White House.

The two had gotten to know each other when Woodward was still a young navy officer and just starting to think about becoming a reporter. They'd met by accident in a waiting room, and during their conversation Woodward asked for advice. In the years since that chance meeting, they'd kept in touch and formed a friendship.

Soon after the Watergate break-in, Bob Woodward talked to his friend. He was willing to help, but Woodward had to agree that he would never for any reason give anyone his friend's name. Ever. Additionally, Woodward could only make contact if it was very important. Even then, they would have to be careful. MF—*my friend*, as Woodward identified the source in his notes—did not give the reporter information directly. Instead, he let Woodward know whether he was on the right track as he followed the evidence.

At first, the two talked by phone. But as the summer wore on and the Watergate story grew more complicated and serious by the day, MF insisted they meet in person and secretly. Woodward should use the back stairs at his apartment building, MF said. Then he should walk through alleys, go in the opposite direction of their meeting place, take a cab partway, then get another cab, and walk the last couple of blocks. Their meeting time and place? Usually two in the morning in an underground garage on the other side of the Potomac River in Virginia.

It sounded silly—like playing hide-and-seek or cops and robbers. But MF wasn't a person who played games or scared easily. And since people at CRP knew about Woodward and Bernstein doing interviews at night, and the people they interviewed were all a pile of nerves, Woodward went along with MF's plan. When he needed to talk, he moved a flowerpot to the front of his apartment balcony as a signal. That night he would sneak to the garage and find MF waiting belowground, usually smoking a

The parking garage in Rosslyn, Virginia, where Bob Woodward met with MF in the middle of the night

cigarette.[27] Woodward never saw anyone watching his balcony and had no idea how MF always knew when he had moved the flowerpot. However strange the arrangement was, though, MF steered Woodward in the right direction every time.

In mid-September Carl Bernstein caught an enormous break. It took way too many cups of coffee one evening, but while he kept swallowing and asking for more, he was able to keep a new and very nervous source talking. She worked in CRP's accounting office—the people who keep track of money going in and out.

At first she wanted nothing to do with Bernstein. She had talked to the FBI and the prosecutors, but ... Bernstein kept at it, sympathizing with her fear. Finally, she opened up.

"I'm an accountant," she said. "Apolitical [not interested in politics]. I didn't do anything wrong. But in some way, something is rotten ... and I'm part of it."[28]

Bernstein drove straight to Woodward's apartment—he was too jumpy to say much on the phone. They put on some music and turned the volume way up. Then Bernstein started talking through his notes while Woodward typed. Even with the music on, neither ever said the woman's name out loud—just in case the apartment was bugged.

CRP had a secret stash of money, hundreds of thousands of dollars, kept in a safe in the office of a Nixon aide, the woman had told Bernstein. Chunks of that money went to several men involved in the Watergate burglary. Her story was huge, bigger than anything the reporters had learned earlier. But only *if* they could confirm that it was true.

Two days later, Woodward's friend MF said that Bernstein's information about the money in a safe was accurate. It had paid for the burglary. But more of that money was used for activities that weren't part of the break-in.

Woodward and Bernstein had wondered back in June if there were incidents other than the Watergate burglary. Now MF had told them that there were. And he confirmed information about where the money for the burglary had come from. But only the actual burglars and their handlers had been formally accused of crimes. Why didn't the men who handed money to the burglars face charges too?

Two weeks earlier, the president had held a news conference. He called the Watergate burglary a "bizarre incident" and assured the press that "no one on the White House staff, no one in this administration, presently employed, was involved." He went on, his voice calm and serious like a father sharing advice with a child. ". . . over-zealous people in campaigns sometimes do things that are wrong. What really hurts is if you try to cover it up."[29]

Once again, the two reporters thought Nixon had chosen his words carefully: "no one presently employed." They could think of at least five key Nixon aides who'd been involved in Watergate in some way. And MF had told Woodward that it was aides to John Mitchell, head of CRP and former attorney general, who controlled the secret fund. None of those men were still employed by either CRP or the White House.

CHAPTER 5

Exercising the First Amendment
SEPTEMBER–NOVEMBER 1972

B y mid-September most Americans didn't care to read or listen to news about Watergate anymore. After all, wasn't the whole thing just politics as usual? A young man named Hugh Sloan didn't think so. Not at all.

Bob Woodward and Carl Bernstein met Sloan as part of their investigation of the $25,000 check. They actually found the former CRP treasurer quite likable. Sloan was in his early thirties and soft-spoken. He said he'd been a White House staffer and then moved to the Committee to Reelect the President.

Hugh Sloan came to Washington to work in the Nixon administration because he believed in the president's promises. The job with CRP was a great way to help make sure Richard Nixon had the chance to follow through on his platform. But soon after the Watergate break-in Sloan resigned, refusing to be part of anything dishonest or illegal. When he first talked to Woodward and Bernstein,

The reporters agreed with Nixon that the break-in was a "bizarre incident." But if someone in the campaign was simply carried away with enthusiasm and that alone explained the burglary, why were the reporters finding so much other information? Why were their sources terrified of even saying a name out loud? And why hadn't the FBI's investigation gotten to the bottom of the story?

Seven weeks before the presidential election, something in Washington—something at the highest level of government—was terribly, terribly wrong. Yet only the *Washington Post* and a few other news outlets around the country still reported on the story regularly or in any detail. On August 22, a front-page story by Woodward and Bernstein started, "The Government Accounting Office has discovered violations in the handling of nearly $500,000 of campaign contributions . . ."

The next day's top headline read, "Nixon Nominated for Second Term." That was the story most news outlets carried.

Hugh Sloan, treasurer for the Committee to Reelect the President, resigned from the committee rather than do anything illegal.

he'd been unemployed for two months and his wife was expecting their first baby very soon.

Bernstein thought Sloan's eyes showed sadness, not anger, and he was a bit too thin. The young man told Bernstein that a lot of people at the White House believed in the law and in following the rules. But they'd convinced themselves that it was okay to break those rules in order to see their mission through. That mission, of course, was the success of Richard Nixon's presidency and the peace he had promised. Sloan realized that people who work at the White House can lose their way very easily, he told the reporters. In all the importance of working for the president, they start feeling special and can forget that they and the president work for the American people. Sloan was hurt and disillusioned by what he'd seen.

A few weeks later, near the end of September, just after his daughter was born, Sloan talked to Bernstein and Woodward again. He said he had managed the money that came out of the secret fund starting in 1971. At first he thought the money was for legal campaign expenses. But after a while, the secrecy and the way the money was handled led him to "assume the worst."[30] He worried that the money and the activities it paid for were illegal. Every time someone asked for money from the fund, Sloan said, he had to get approval from a person higher up. At the beginning, in 1971, that person was John Mitchell.

Bernstein and Woodward were afraid to breathe. They stopped Sloan to be sure they'd heard him correctly. They had. In 1971, though, John Mitchell was not the head of the Committee to Reelect the President. That would be bad enough. But in 1971, Mitchell was still the attorney general of the United States—the nation's highest law enforcement official and a member of the president's cabinet. John Mitchell ran the Department of Justice and at the very same time, according to Hugh Sloan, he approved spending illegal campaign funds on illegal or unethical activities designed to harm the president's opponents.

How many broken laws did Hugh Sloan acknowledge?

Many. First, the laws of the early 1970s made hiding campaign donations a crime no matter what a campaign used the money for. Second, many of the activities those funds financed were crimes—things like breaking and entering, bugging phones without a warrant, paying people to break the law, and more. Third, as attorney general, John Mitchell took an oath to enforce federal laws and investigate possible violations of federal laws—including campaign finance laws. His job also included overseeing federal prosecutors all over the country as they went after those who broke federal laws. But if Sloan was right, Mitchell was breaking the very laws he had sworn to enforce. That's quite a lot to think about.

Late that night, Carl Bernstein finished the article he and Bob Woodward had written. As reporters do, he called a CRP press official for a comment or response to the article, which he would include with the piece. Then he called John Mitchell himself for comment and read him the opening sentence:

> John N. Mitchell, while serving as US Attorney
> General, personally controlled a secret Repub-
> lican fund that was used to gather information
> about the Democrats . . .

Mitchell started yelling, sounding like someone in terrible pain. He shouted again and again as Bernstein kept
reading. Before the end of the first paragraphs, the former
attorney general cut Bernstein off, saying, "All that crap,
you're putting it in the paper? It's all been denied. Katie
Graham's gonna get . . . caught in a big, fat wringer if
that's published."

John Mitchell had just threatened Katharine Graham,
the owner and publisher of the *Washington Post*. Bernstein took notes as fast as he could. Finally, Mitchell
said, ". . . we're going to do a story on all of *you*."[31]

Bernstein felt shaken and shocked at the ugliness of
Mitchell's rage, at his screaming into the phone. At his
threats. What story could there be on the *Washington Post*
or its people? Everything the paper had reported on Watergate was true. And who did Mitchell mean by *we*? For now,
it didn't matter. What mattered was getting the story out.

The Watergate story was different from anything Carl
Bernstein or Bob Woodward had ever worked on before,

and it carried a huge responsibility. If they got it wrong, their careers could be over. Worse, if they accused an innocent person, it could destroy that person's career. And if they fell for false information, it could ruin the *Washington Post*. The worry had kept Carl Bernstein awake at night. The former attorney general's threats didn't help.

The *Washington Post* took accuracy and reliability very seriously. Like all good and reputable news organizations, the *Post* had strict rules about the stories they published. When it came to Watergate, the *Post*'s owner and editors made the rules even stricter. Nothing in a story would go to print without at least two sources saying it was accurate. If information could harm someone's career or reputation, the editors sometimes asked for three or more sources. And one or more of the paper's chief editors read every Watergate article carefully before it went to print. Even so, the reporters worried about making a mistake. They agreed that if either one of them was unsure about a story, the story would not go to press.

Are all news articles just facts? Or do some articles include journalists' opinions?

Reliable, professionally run news organizations separate straight news from opinion. On the front page of a newspaper or at the beginning of a television or radio newscast, the stories stick to the facts—who, what, when, where, why, or how. Journalists write those pieces to inform the public. The readers or viewer can then draw their own conclusions. Other journalists, known as columnists or commentators, give their opinions in a separate section of the paper called the editorial or op-ed page or at the end of a newscast. Responsible news organizations make the difference between just-the-facts news and opinion pieces very clear to the reader, viewer, or listener. And they are careful to present opinion pieces from well-informed people or experts on different sides of an issue.

Late one evening near the end of September, Carl Bernstein got a call from a government lawyer whose work had nothing to do with Watergate. But, the man said, a friend had told him something very odd that might be helpful to Bernstein. Bernstein started typing. As with many pieces of the Watergate puzzle that he and Bob Woodward had uncovered over the summer, they still had more questions than answers. With luck, this lawyer might open some new doors for them.

A year earlier in 1971, the lawyer said, someone in Nixon's campaign had offered his friend a job. The campaign was hiring people to upset, interrupt, and damage Democratic candidates' primary campaigns. The idea was to hurt all the Democratic candidates, especially any candidates who had a real chance of beating Richard Nixon in November 1972.

Bernstein, Woodward, a reporter in California where the lawyer's friend lived, and several other people at the *Post* took what the lawyer told Bernstein and started searching for more details. Over the next ten days, they discovered that the story was not only true, but that it was far bigger than the lawyer had realized, and the FBI knew about it. Woodward took the information to MF, who confirmed everything and for the first time, gave the reporter new details. Woodward and Bernstein's lead article, followed by two more articles, spread across the front page of the *Washington Post* on October 10, less than one month before the election.

FBI Finds Nixon Aides Sabotaged Democrats . . .

FBI agents have established that the Watergate bugging incident stemmed from a massive campaign of political spying and sabotage conducted on behalf of President Nixon's reelection and directed by officials of the White House . . .

For the first time, the disaster of the Democrats' campaign over the last year made sense. Most people thought of politics as a dirty sort of business. But they'd had no idea a campaign would sink this low. The articles revealed that a White House aide had forged the letter that played a big part in ending Senator Ed Muskie's campaign. The same White House aide made up the accusations against Mrs. Muskie. Additionally, the Nixon team had hired at least fifty people to travel the country disrupting and spying on Democratic candidates in the "dirty tricks" campaign they'd been so careful to keep secret. And the person who made the job offer to the young man in California had promised him unlimited funds to carry out the dirty tricks as well as a "good government job" as a reward after Nixon won the election. The whole thing was one big operation under the direction of men at the White House and at CRP. The money for it came from the enormous and illegal secret fund the *Post* had reported on earlier. People paying attention were shocked.

But if FBI officials knew all of this and it was "part of the Watergate investigation,"[32] why weren't more people going to jail? And what did the White House have to say about it?

The president and his aides didn't defend themselves with facts. Instead, they attacked the news outlets that reported on the story, often in televised news conferences that appeared nationwide. Nixon's press secretary said the *Washington Post*'s articles were based on *hearsay, innuendo,* and *unsubstantiated* charges. A Republican senator called the *Post*'s stories *political garbage.* Nixon's campaign chairman used words like *malicious* and *hypocrisy.*

The majority of the American people either ignored or never saw the print news stories and leaned toward believing that the *Washington Post* and other papers were unfair and their articles were inaccurate or downright fake news. *Post* Executive Editor Ben Bradlee responded, saying, "The facts are on the record, unchallenged by contrary evidence."[33] No one had found anything to prove that the *Washington Post*'s Watergate stories were inaccurate. But that didn't stop the attacks from the White House.

Bradlee told Woodward and Bernstein, "This is the hardest hardball that's ever been played in this town. We all have to be very careful, in the office and out."

He warned the reporters to be cautious about whom they talked to, whom they were seen with, what they said on the phone, and what they said about the president.[34] They didn't tell him they were already doing all that. Hearing the warnings from someone with Ben Bradlee's experience, though, was chilling. Over the next few weeks, Woodward and Bernstein found no evidence that their phones were bugged or that they faced any real threat, and they relaxed a little.[35] But they remained cautious in what they said and whom they talked to. They didn't want to take chances or give White House aides any real reason to attack them.

The *Washington Post*'s Watergate articles continued, as did articles in the *New York Times* and *Los Angeles Times* and a few other papers and magazines. The White House attacks on the press—still without evidence—continued as well. In the last week of October, Woodward and Bernstein reported another bombshell.

The reporters knew that John Mitchell wasn't the only person who okayed the money coming out of the secret fund. In late October, Hugh Sloan told Woodward and Bernstein that the president's chief of staff and closest aide, Bob Haldeman, was one of the men who controlled the fund as well.

As chief of staff, Haldeman spent hours with the president almost every day, advised the president on all sorts of issues, decided who could speak with the president and who couldn't, and far more. But at the same time, according to Sloan, he had approved the use of illegally gathered money from an illegal secret fund to pay for unethical and sometimes illegal activities—just as the attorney general had. Woodward and Bernstein spoke with two other sources who confirmed that Haldeman had authority over the money, and then they wrote the story. They reported that Hugh Sloan had told the prosecutors and the grand jury about Haldeman's role with the secret fund (a grand jury is a special jury that decides if crimes have been committed and if people should be *indicted*, officially accused).

The next morning, a reporter from another section of the paper came to Woodward and shared what he'd heard on the radio on his way into the office. Hugh Sloan did *not* tell the grand jury that Haldeman approved payments from the secret fund. Woodward was so shaken he asked the other reporter to repeat his words. Bob Woodward's knees felt like jelly and he sat down hard. Once he got hold of himself, he went to Bernstein's desk to break the news. Carl Bernstein's face went white and then red. He took several deep breaths as waves of nausea swept over him. They'd been wrong.

This was the very thing that kept Bernstein from sleeping well. And now it had happened. His reputation and Woodward's were on the line. Their careers as journalists could be over. But that was nothing compared to what their mistake might do to the *Washington Post*. The White House would use a mistake like this as a weapon to say

The Washington Post Building on 15th Street in
Washington, DC

everything the *Post* had reported was suspect. The paper
could lose readers and advertisers. It could lose the public
trust. And what about Bob Haldeman? Had they wrongly
accused him of illegal and unethical behavior?

The usually bustling, noisy newsroom fell silent as if
everyone had just heard news of a death. Woodward and
Bernstein were near panic. They had to find out just how

bad their mistake was. How much had they gotten wrong? And how? They called Sloan's number but got no answer. They called again and then again. Nothing. Should they resign immediately? Should they issue an apology to Haldeman—a man everyone in Washington seemed to fear? And why wouldn't Sloan answer their calls?

Ben Bradlee looked as sick about the mistake as the reporters did. But until they all knew exactly what had happened, he was sticking by Woodward and Bernstein. They'd earned his trust over the last four months. In the meantime, he had to make a statement for publication. Bradlee turned to his typewriter. His statement was one sentence—"We stand by our story."

Woodward and Bernstein kept trying to get in touch with Hugh Sloan or his lawyer. This was personal as well as professional. They liked Sloan and had developed his trust. The last thing they wanted to do was hurt his reputation. They also called their other sources, and Woodward let MF know he needed a meeting.

After several days of detective work, no sleep, terrible nerves, and a very tense meeting with Woodward's friend, the reporters finally pieced it together. Yes, Sloan had told them that Haldeman controlled the secret fund. And yes, he had talked to the prosecutors and the grand jury. But Woodward and Bernstein had assumed incorrectly that

Sloan had told the grand jury the same thing he told them. He didn't tell the prosecutors or the grand jury about Haldeman's role because they didn't ask if Haldeman was involved. They didn't ask who controlled the money.

The reporters had made a mistake and would print a correction. But the major information in the *Post* story, the real point of the story, was accurate. Definitely and absolutely. Haldeman had controlled the secret fund.

Woodward and Bernstein were relieved, and Katharine Graham agreed with Ben Bradlee that the two should not resign. The reporters knew they'd let down everyone at the *Washington Post*. They wouldn't let them down again. For now, though, with one week left until the presidential election, they needed to get back to work. Someone still had to get to the bottom of Watergate.

Bob Woodward and Carl Bernstein expected the attacks on the *Post* and on them to lighten up once the election was over. Everyone knew Nixon was going to win, and after he did, there would be no point in accusing the reporters of working for the Democrats as they continued to cover Watergate. They didn't know about Richard Nixon's plans to ruin his enemies, the *Washington Post* among them.

In the few weeks after Nixon's reelection, *Washington Post* reporters who covered things like social events and

ceremonies at the White House found they were no longer invited to those functions. The White House had
banned *Washington Post* reporters altogether. No one in the
administration would talk to anyone from the *Washington
Post* for any reason, political or nonpolitical. *Post* reporters who'd covered White House events for decades were
caught off guard. They'd never experienced anything like
this no matter what the political news was. And the new
White House policy would hurt the *Post* if it went on
for a long time. Washingtonians who liked reading about
White House parties and dinners and who now had to
find articles in the *Post*'s competition, the *Washington Star*,
might cancel their subscriptions to the *Post*. If subscriptions went down, businesses that paid to put advertise-
ments in the *Post* might go elsewhere. The *Post* couldn't
afford to lose that subscription and advertising income for
any length of time.

The *Washington Star* responded to the White House
boycott of the *Post* with an editorial defending the First
Amendment—if the *Post*'s reporters couldn't cover White
House social events, their reporters wouldn't either. Katharine Graham called the editorial the "most generous minded
statement I can imagine in behalf of the competition."[36]

A few days later, Carl Bernstein had dinner with a
Washington Star reporter and other friends. The reporter

shared pieces of a conversation he'd had with a White House aide just before the election. The aide had said,

> As soon as the election is behind us, we're [the White House] going to really shove it to the *Post* . . . the basic decisions have been made—at a meeting with the president. . . . They're [people at the *Washington Post*] going to wish . . . they'd never heard of Watergate.[37]

The First Amendment was under attack, but it would still protect the *Washington Post* from being officially shut down by the government. And the *Star* had been generous in defending the *Post* and freedom of the press. But a few weeks later, the situation worsened.

Like most big newspapers, the *Washington Post* was one piece of a larger company that also owned magazines and television stations. The income from those businesses helped support the newspaper. Now the entire company came under attack.

Television stations must get a license to operate from the Federal Communications Commission, an agency of the executive branch of government, and they must renew that license every few years. At the end of December 1972, several business executives challenged the *Post*'s television

The US Constitution's First Amendment, part of the Bill of Rights, guarantees freedom of the press

licenses in Florida. They asked the FCC not to renew the licenses, but let them, the executives, buy them instead. Katharine Graham couldn't think of any good reason for the FCC to deny the licenses' renewal. The stations had always followed all the FCC rules and regulations for television broadcasting. They'd earned top ratings for excellent news coverage and community service, too. She also found it suspicious that no other station in Florida had been challenged. Only the two owned by the *Post*.

Graham wasn't certain her paper could survive if she lost those television licenses. Television stations can charge much more for TV commercials than a newspaper

Katharine Graham, owner and publisher of the
Washington Post, was the first American woman in
the twentieth century to serve as publisher of a major
newspaper.

can for ads in print. Those stations brought more money
to the *Washington Post* Company than a newspaper ever
could no matter how good it was. When Graham learned
the names of the men who wanted to gain control of the

stations, she had no doubt what was happening. They were wealthy friends and supporters of Richard Nixon. No one could find solid proof that Nixon had encouraged his friends to go after the *Post*'s licenses, but it certainly looked as though the president of the United States was using an executive branch agency and his friends to ruin an "enemy."

Katharine Graham worried about all the people who worked for her at the *Washington Post*. But she wasn't about to give in to Richard Nixon's threats. She wasn't going to tell her editors to back off or not print well-researched facts about the Nixon administration. She would defend her right to keep the television stations (she won, but the legal battle eventually cost the *Washington Post* Company over a million dollars). And she would try to find a way for the paper to survive financially in the meantime.[38] The *Washington Post* had to keep reporting the news as the editors saw fit—just as the First Amendment guarantees. How else would Americans know the truth of what their government was doing?

CHAPTER 6

An Angry Judge
NOVEMBER 1972–MARCH 1973

President Nixon hoped that the January trial of the Watergate burglars would end the story once and for all. He and his men felt very good about the judge who'd been on the case from the start. John Sirica was a conservative like they were, and he'd been very active in the Republican Party before becoming a judge. In fact, people said those Republican connections got him an appointment as a judge in the first place. Nixon and his aides were confident that Sirica would "take their side" even though judges aren't supposed to take sides.

Judge John Sirica was the chief judge of the federal court in Washington, DC, part of the judicial branch of government. He'd overseen the Watergate burglars case since the summer. In September, after the FBI finished its investigation, the grand jury had decided that the five burglars and their two handlers should be formally accused and should face trial. But trials don't happen right away since courtrooms are busy and lawyers need time to prepare. Judge

John J. Sirica, chief judge of the US District Court for the District of Columbia, presided over the Watergate case.

Sirica scheduled the Watergate burglary trial for *after* the November election. Exactly what the Nixon team wanted.

But isn't a jury part of the trial? What's this about a *grand* jury?

Most people think of a jury as the group of citizens who sit to one side of a courtroom, listen to the evidence and arguments on both sides of a case, and decide whether the person accused of a crime is guilty or not guilty. That's what a *trial* jury—also called a *petit* jury—does in a criminal case. But there is more than one kind of jury. A grand jury (grand meaning large) is also a group of citizens, but they do not sit in on a trial. The grand jury does its job long before a trial takes place.

Federal prosecutors and their teams investigate crimes and build cases. Then they present the evidence to a grand jury. The grand jury, made up of sixteen to twenty-three citizens called for jury duty, listens to the prosecuting attorney's evidence, and to the witnesses the prosecutor brings in. There is no judge involved, no defense attorney, and the evidence and testimony are kept secret from the press and the public in order to protect the accused and the witnesses. When the prosecutor finishes presenting the case, the grand jury decides whether there is good reason to formally accuse or *indict* the person or persons suspected of committing the crime. If the grand jury does indict a suspect, that person will go to trial. The indictment and the trial are made public.

Americans tend to focus on their *rights* as citizens, but citizens also have *responsibilities*. One of those is serving on a jury when called upon. Other responsibilities include voting (also a right) and paying taxes.

Sirica wasn't one of those rich-family, elite, Ivy League lawyers or judges Nixon despised. John Sirica had grown up poor in a two-room apartment with his immigrant parents. As a teenager, he worked for a garbage collector to help his family pay the bills. Eventually, he went to Georgetown University Law School while earning tuition money as a boxing instructor. He even boxed professionally for a short time before practicing law. That was the kind of toughness Nixon admired.

But John Sirica was more than tough and a conservative. He also believed wholeheartedly in the law. As the trial date drew nearer, he surprised Nixon and his men.

Judge Sirica hadn't been happy during the summer with the testimony that the government prosecutors presented to the grand jury. Sure, their evidence showed that a crime occurred and that the seven men charged should be indicted. But the judge knew that those seven men weren't the whole story. He wanted to know why the government's lawyers weren't going deeper.

In early December, Sirica told the prosecutors, "The jury is going to want to know." Jurors in the January trial would want to know who hired the burglars. They'd want to know what the point of the break-in was and how the men were paid. Most of all, the jury was going to want to know who proposed the break-in and who okayed the idea.[39] Sirica had the same kinds of questions Woodward and Bernstein and other reporters had been trying to answer. But nothing the prosecutors had presented to the grand jury came close to explaining any of it.

The trial of the seven indicted men started on January 8. As soon as the lawyers finished their opening statements, Howard Hunt, one of the two burglary handlers, asked to plead guilty. Two days later, the four burglars from Miami did the same thing. Pleading guilty meant that the men admitted committing the crimes they were charged with— breaking and entering, stealing documents, planting telephone taps and bugs, and more. It also meant that there was no longer any reason to go through with a trial. And no reason for the government's lawyers to question them in front of the jury and try to get to the bottom of the story.

At the same time, the *New York Times* reported that "at least four of the five men arrested ... in the Watergate raid are still being paid by persons as yet unnamed. ..."[40] Paid for what? To plead guilty and stay quiet? The four Miami burglars and Hunt could have pleaded guilty long before the trial actually started. They could have pleaded guilty the day the grand jury indicted them or any time after that. But they hadn't. Why now?

The next day, Woodward and Bernstein reported in the *Washington Post* that Howard Hunt had pressured the other four men to plead guilty. He said their families would "be taken care of" while they served short prison sentences.[41] Judge Sirica knew what the *Times* and *Post* articles said. But the men denied there had been any pressure or bribes even when Sirica told them that he was likely to give them the longest prison sentences he could.

The guilty pleas left only two men facing the jury—James McCord, the burglar who had worked for the CIA and owned a security company, and Gordon Liddy, a former FBI agent and one of the burglary handlers. Judge Sirica was angry and frustrated that the whole truth might never come out.

Meanwhile, Richard Nixon was inaugurated president for a second term on January 20. Polls showed that nearly 70 percent of Americans approved of him and the job he was doing. They still didn't think Watergate was worth all the fuss newspapers made over it. The *Washington Post* hadn't slowed down its coverage of the story at all, and the *New York Times*, *Los Angeles Times*, *Time* and *Newsweek* magazines, and major television networks had increased theirs. But the majority of Americans weren't paying close attention.

Sirica, on the other hand, believed the fuss was well-deserved. As the trial went on, his anger with the prosecutors, the witnesses, and the two remaining defendants grew.

Richard Nixon takes the oath of office from Chief Justice Warren Burger as First Lady Pat Nixon looks on, January 20, 1973.

Their questions and answers were simply inadequate. More than once he sent the jury into another room and quizzed witnesses himself. Where did the money come from? What was the money used for? Who was in charge?

John Sirica was a solidly built man with a nose shaped by his days as a boxer. He wore his salt-and-pepper hair slicked straight back and had a deep crease between his thick brows. Judge Sirica could be an intimidating figure and knew how to make a defendant's knees shake. But nothing he did during the two-week trial made any difference. The men would not open up.

The jury convicted both McCord and Liddy on all charges. But none of the seven men, not one, had given the court any answers at all about who was behind the break-in. Worse, Judge Sirica was very sure that they had all lied under oath, committed *perjury*, a serious crime that can result in prison time. After the jury announced the guilty verdict, Sirica told the prosecutors,

> I have not been satisfied, and I am still not satisfied that all the ... facts that might be available ... have been produced before an American jury.[42]

Bob Woodward and Carl Bernstein reported in the *Washington Post* the next morning:

> Still Secret: Who Hired Spies and Why
> The Watergate bugging trial was marked by questions not asked of witnesses, answers not given, witnesses not called to testify and some lapses of [gaps in] memory by those testifying under oath.[43]

The *Los Angeles Times* said:

> The questioning of Republican officials has been
> more polite than penetrating. Entire areas have
> been left unprobed.[44]

Three days later, Sirica again met the defendants in
court to decide if he would grant bail and release them
while they waited to hear their sentences. He told them
that he would make his sentencing decision in a few
weeks. The judge hoped the seven men knew of his reputation for giving long sentences. He wanted them to think
about that for a while.

The Senate had just announced that it would open its
own investigation into Watergate. The convicted burglary
team was sure to be called to testify. Sirica suggested that
if the burglars chose to come clean and tell the Senate the
truth, the *whole* truth, perhaps he would decide on shorter
prison terms for them.

Then he spoke to everyone in the courtroom—lawyers,
defendants, reporters, and others.

> Everybody knows there's going to be a Congres-
> sional [Senate] investigation in this case. I would
> hope, frankly—not only as a judge but as a citizen

of a great country . . . I would hope that the Senate committee is granted power by Congress . . .
to get to the bottom of what happened . . .[45]

Sirica waited until late March to call the men back to
court for sentencing. They'd had plenty of time to think
about prison. Reporters crammed into the courtroom
benches where the jury sat for trials and every seat in the
public section of the room was taken. Everyone quieted
as the clock approached ten. Then the bailiff called, "All
rise." People stood in a whoosh of motion as Judge John
Sirica entered and moved toward the bench. He sat and
everyone followed with another whoosh.

"Prior to the beginning of the sentencing," he said
in a deep voice that carried to the back of the room, "I
wish to put a certain important matter on record in open
court."

Spectators looked at one another. What was going on?
This wasn't how sentencing hearings typically worked.
The only sound in the courtroom was the crinkle of
paper as Sirica unfolded a letter from James McCord.
Judge Sirica began reading aloud. McCord's letter
started with an explanation of his decision to send such a
letter to the judge. He wrote that his family was afraid he
would be murdered if he told all he knew. He was afraid

that his honesty would put friends and family in danger of losing their jobs or having their reputations ruined with lies. But he'd decided to go forward anyway, he said, in an attempt to repair some of the damage he and the others had caused to the justice system. McCord then listed facts he wanted the judge to know.

1. There was political pressure applied to the defendants to plead guilty and remain silent.

2. Perjury occurred during the trial . . .

3. Others involved in the Watergate operation were not identified during the trial, when they could have been by those testifying.

4. The Watergate operation was not a CIA operation [though] the Cubans [from Miami] may have been misled by others . . .

The letter went on and then finished with McCord saying that he could not "feel confident" talking to the FBI or to government lawyers or to other government officials.[46] To Judge Sirica, the last part of the letter meant that McCord knew the cover-up was so big that he couldn't trust anyone in the executive branch, not even the FBI or Justice Department prosecutors.

The courtroom erupted with everyone whispering,

reporters trying to get to the doors to call their news-rooms, and the bailiff banging his gavel. No one noticed that Judge Sirica was struggling as he finished reading. He had called a brief *recess* or break and gone to his chambers (office). The judge had a sharp pain in his chest, a pain that built while he read McCord's letter, but started to fade after he lay down for a few minutes. His doctor later determined that fatigue and nervous tension had caused the chest pain. The trial was making the judge sick.

Fifteen minutes later, after the pain lessened, Sirica returned to the courtroom. He told McCord he would think about the letter and sentence him at another time. As for the others, he gave each of them the longest sentence possible under the law.

That wasn't the end of the case for the burglars. The grand jury was not finished with its Watergate work. There was more evidence and other possible crimes to consider. The convicted men could be called to testify about new information. And the Senate would want to talk to them as well. Sirica looked at the men, his face deadly serious. "I recommend your full cooperation with the grand jury and the Senate Select Committee." Once again, he reminded everyone that he could not promise anything, but there would be an opportunity for him to rethink their sentences.[47]

A lawyer named Sam Dash sat in the front row watching and listening. Dash hadn't been involved in the Watergate story in any way until late January as the burglary trial ended. But he was about to become a key figure in pushing the system of checks and balances forward. What he'd just witnessed in Judge John Sirica's courtroom gave him pause. He said later, "It looked like Watergate was about to break wide open."[48]

CHAPTER 7

The Senate Steps In

MARCH–MAY 1973

S amuel Dash knew a lot about doing research. He'd been researching legal issues for most of his adult life. But this new job, chief counsel (head lawyer) for the Senate Select Committee on Presidential Campaign Activities, was his biggest research project yet. He needed to get to work fast.

The Senate Select Committee on Presidential Campaign Activities? That's a mouthful. Was the Senate investigating Watergate or not?

Yes and no. Both the US Senate and the House of Representatives use committees to conduct much of their work. Each committee focuses on a specific issue or set of policies. Permanent, or *standing*, committees work on issues in agriculture, foreign affairs, and more. A bill or proposed law cannot go to a vote by the whole Senate or House unless the appropriate committee approves it first. Senate and House members generally serve on more than one standing committee and often become experts on the areas those committees cover (unfortunately, that is not always so). Every committee has a mix of Democrats and Republicans.

Senate and House members also serve on *select* committees, which are usually temporary and deal with a single specific problem or issue. The Senate Select Committee on Presidential Campaign Activities had the job of investigating the Watergate affair.

So, the entire Senate was not investigating Watergate—the select committee was.

Most people called it simply the Senate Watergate Committee.

Senators had followed the newspaper investigations of Watergate all summer and through the fall of 1972. The *Washington Post*'s reporting, particularly the almost daily articles by Woodward and Bernstein, gave several senators serious concerns about the way the Department of Justice was handling the Watergate case—the same concerns Judge John Sirica had. Just before the burglary trial started in early January 1973, senators began discussing how to organize their own investigation. On February 7,

Members of the Senate Watergate Committee (left to right): Howard Baker (TN), Herman Talmadge (GA), Joseph Montoya (NM), Sam Dash (majority counsel), Sam Ervin (NC, seated), Daniel Inouye (HI), Fred Thompson (minority counsel), Lowell Weicker (CT)

less than a week after the trial ended, the Senate voted unanimously to create a select committee of four Democrats and three Republicans. The committee would hire research and office staff to assist them.

The Senate Watergate Committee had a very specific

mission. Investigate the Watergate bugging and its funding, purpose, planning, and guidance—things that the prosecutors in the Watergate burglary case had not presented to the grand jury or at the burglary trial.

The Senate appointed Sam Ervin, a Democratic senator from North Carolina, to chair the committee. It was Ervin who hired Sam Dash as chief counsel. Dash would give legal advice to the members of the Senate committee and oversee the necessary research. He and his staff had to know everything about the complicated case so they could help the committee members ask their witnesses the right questions when the time came. It wasn't a job Dash had applied for or even thought about. But when Ervin asked him to take the job, he knew it was too important to say no.

What was the point of the Senate doing its own investigation?

The Senate does not hand down indictments like a grand jury, or decide if an ordinary person accused of a crime is guilty or not guilty the way a trial jury does. Those are judicial branch jobs. But the Senate and the House write the laws. If the country needed new or stronger campaign laws to avoid another Watergate, the legislative branch had to write them.

And legislators (members of Congress) couldn't do their job well unless they knew what had happened and how it had happened.

Additionally, the Senate has *oversight* responsibilities. After making the laws, Congress must make sure that the executive branch is carrying out the laws as intended. This is part of the system of checks and balances. Sam Dash later explained, the Senate committee had the "duty to inform the public of wrongdoing in the Executive Branch."[49]

Sam Dash brought great experience and expertise to his new job. He'd grown up in Philadelphia during the Great Depression with immigrant parents who he described as "dirt poor." They valued education, and after serving as a bombardier navigator during World War II, Dash graduated from Temple University at the top of his class and then went to Harvard University Law School. Five years later, he became a district attorney or chief prosecutor for the City of Philadelphia and later researched and cowrote a book on the technology and use of electronic surveillance such as wiretapping and bugging. In 1973 he was teaching criminal law at Georgetown University Law School and directing a research institute there. No one had better qualifications for advising the Senate committee.

On the day that Judge Sirica read McCord's letter to the courtroom, Sam Dash was still trying to get his new office up and running. He needed a big staff of energetic young lawyers, researchers, and investigators who were eager to spend every waking hour in a windowless auditorium sifting through thousands of pages of documents. He needed people who knew how to organize such a mound of information so they could find any piece of it quickly (only a few offices used computers in 1973 and laptops, tablets, the Internet, and smartphones didn't yet exist). In fact, Dash made this the first Congressional investigation to use computers—without them, the staff would drown in information. Soon, he had nearly a hundred people working for him.

The Senate committee planned to hold hearings to formally question witnesses once Dash and his team completed investigations in three areas: the Watergate break-in and cover-up, political spying and sabotage of opponents' campaigns, and violations of campaign finance laws.[50] The McCord letter made the break-in and cover-up, especially the cover-up, the highest priority. Everything else could wait.

Dash hurried back to his office after the sentencing hearing and found a phone message on his desk. James McCord wanted to talk. The Senate investigation had begun.

* * *

McCord told Dash that the deputy-chairman of CRP had lied under oath during the trial when he said that he knew nothing about the burglary or buggings before the arrests at the Watergate. According to McCord, the man did know about the whole thing ahead of time and had even been in on the planning. Furthermore, President Nixon's counsel (lawyer), John Dean, was involved as well.

Unbelievable. The *Washington Post* had already reported that former attorney general John Mitchell was involved in the Watergate affair, though it hadn't been proven yet. But Mitchell's top aide? And the president's lawyer? This could be the biggest political scandal in American history.

Dash instructed his staff to talk to the secretaries who worked for the men McCord had named. Like Woodward and Bernstein, they discovered that the FBI had never questioned most of these people in their Watergate investigation. And Dash's team found that the secretaries and other office workers were more than willing to share what they knew. Yes, there had been meetings during the winter of 1972 between Attorney General Mitchell, his aide, White House Counsel John Dean, and Gordon Liddy— one of the men arrested for the break-in four months after the meeting. They'd met in the attorney general's office.

Over several days, Dash spent long hours talking with

James McCord and his lawyer. McCord wanted to tell the committee what he knew despite the threats to himself and his family. Dash liked McCord. It was clear that the former CIA man loved his country and had spent a lifetime protecting it. So how could he have ...

> "Broken into Watergate?" McCord said. "As I now see it for what it was ... I will regret what I did ... for the rest of my life."[51]

Dash realized that James McCord was patriotic and willing to sacrifice for the United States. But the man didn't fully understand the principles of the US Constitution. McCord had forgotten where his loyalty belonged. He broke the law because he thought that's what the White House asked of him. He should have refused because that's what the Constitution he'd sworn to uphold demanded.

How many others had fallen into that trap?

Sam Dash started arriving at his office at six in the morning and heading home around midnight. Even then, he didn't often go right to bed. He read documents and reviewed notes and rarely slept more than three hours. After McCord's letter hit the news, other Watergate figures had decided they should come forward too, as Dash thought they would. The flow of information and accusations he had to absorb became an avalanche.

Hugh Sloan, the former CRP treasurer who'd opened up to Woodward and Bernstein, now told his story again. He'd lost more weight, and his hair showed flecks of gray though he was only in his thirties. Dash thought he was a very good witness. Sloan said that Mitchell's people had tried to convince him to lie to the grand jury. A top official at CRP had suggested he plead the Fifth Amendment, meaning he could refuse to answer questions because his answers might be used as evidence of his guilt. No one in the US can be forced to give evidence of their own guilt in court, but Sloan hadn't broken any laws. He hadn't committed any crimes and had no guilt. He didn't need to plead the Fifth Amendment for himself. It would be just a way to cover up for other people. Sloan wouldn't do that. He told Dash that shortly after he had resigned from CRP the previous summer, he'd gone to the head prosecutor in the Watergate case to report the pressure to commit perjury. But the prosecutor ignored his accusations.

Dash's staff of a hundred lawyers, researchers, and secretaries worked from an auditorium in the basement of the Senate Office Building. It was the only place big enough to hold them and all the boxes upon boxes of documents they had to go through. Day after day, they plugged away while committee members and their aides came in and out, along with witnesses and their lawyers. Reporters also came looking for scoops. The place bustled with activity and noise from early morning until late at night, and almost no one ever took a day off.

But after weeks of hard work and long hours, the staffers were tired and discouraged. It wasn't just the hurried meals and lack of sleep or the constant distractions in the auditorium. The eager young lawyers and researchers had willingly signed on for all that and low pay. But from what they could tell in the spring of 1973, the public had lost any interest in Watergate after the burglary trial ended. Dash's staff had accepted their difficult positions because they wanted to serve their country. But if their country didn't care about Watergate . . .

Sam Dash understood their feelings. He told them that he believed the American people *did* care about corruption in government. They *did* care about bribery and all the other potential crimes in the Nixon administration. They weren't really ignoring the story, Dash said. That wasn't the problem. The problem was that the Watergate story was confusing and complicated (it still is), and people didn't see how it had anything to do with them. Dash was confident that the Senate committee could change that attitude with good support from the chief counsel and his staff. The public *needed* to know what had happened and what was still happening even if they didn't yet understand *why* they needed to know.[52] Dash understood— citizens without knowledge are powerless.

The staffers believed in Dash. They admired his expertise in the law and his own hard work. If he thought their work in the basement auditorium was going to make a real difference, they'd keep at it.

In the last days of April, the press and the president himself got the public's attention again. The *New York Daily News* and then Woodward and Bernstein at the *Washington Post* reported that the acting director of the FBI, the head of the nation's top law enforcement agency, had destroyed documents related to Watergate—documents taken from a safe in the White House. The president's counsel, John Dean, had given the director the documents and told him they "should never see the light of day."[53] They had to remain secret. The director had taken care of it. But destroying evidence in a criminal investigation is a very serious crime. If the director of the FBI had done that, who could Americans trust?

There was more. The director had also kept John Dean

informed of every step in the FBI's Watergate investigation with daily reports, a terrible violation of professional standards. The same day that the article appeared, the FBI director resigned.

Before anyone had time to take a breath, more shocking news came.

Two years earlier, in 1971, a man named Daniel Ellsberg had been arrested and charged with crimes related to espionage. The case had been all over the news at the time. Ellsberg, a Harvard graduate and former marine officer, had spent time in Vietnam with the State Department. He then worked as a researcher on the history of the Vietnam War for the Department of Defense. Ellsberg discovered that the US government and three US presidents had lied to the American people about the war in Vietnam for almost twenty years. He tried to convince key members of Congress to use the report as they made decisions about Richard Nixon's continuation of the war. Congress took no action. Ellsberg, determined to let the American people know about the report, then shared parts of the document with a few carefully chosen people outside government, including a reporter from the *New York Times*. In June 1971, the *New York Times* began publishing sections of the seven-thousand-page report. Days later, the *Washington Post* published other pieces of it and then more went to sev-

Daniel Ellsberg speaks to the press. Espionage and other charges against Ellsberg were dropped in May 1972.

eral other newspapers around the country. Richard Nixon tried to stop the newspapers from publishing the report—known as the Pentagon Papers—but the Supreme Court ruled against him. Under the First Amendment, the papers could publish the material since Ellsberg had kept back any information that would harm current national defense (this became part of Richard Nixon's grudge against the *New York Times* and the *Washington Post* two years later). But the

Supreme Court ruling didn't excuse Ellsberg's theft of the Defense Department report.

Now in the spring of 1973, Ellsberg was finally on trial in California. He faced many years in prison if a jury convicted him of espionage. But in April, as Dash's team probed Watergate and the *Washington Post* and *New York Times* kept up their reporting on the White House, the judge in the Ellsberg trial stopped everything. He had learned that two of the men convicted in the Watergate burglary—Gordon Liddy and Howard Hunt—had also burglarized a doctor's office in California. They'd been trying to steal Ellsberg's medical records in hope of finding something that would make him look untrustworthy or unstable when he went to trial. Something that might keep the jury and the public from believing his testimony. The judge said the attempt to smear Ellsberg, as well as other "improper government conduct" in the case, offended a "sense of justice."[54] He *dismissed* or threw out Ellsberg's case and dropped all the charges against him. Daniel Ellsberg would go free.

Stealing and exposing someone's private medical records? Americans didn't like that idea at all, no matter what they thought of Daniel Ellsberg. And the same burglars who bungled the Watergate break-in? Who authorized these things? Who even thought of them?

And how far did this kind of illegal activity go?

Next, the *Washington Post* reported that the president's counsel, John Dean, planned to admit his own criminal guilt. He was talking to government prosecutors. The Watergate grand jury that had indicted the five burglars and their handlers was still at work in late April. The burglars had been convicted in February, but now the grand jury was hearing evidence on other parts of the Watergate story. Dean planned to testify that Nixon's top aides— Bob Haldeman and John Ehrlichman—were in on the Watergate cover-up just as he was. Was that possible?

A partial answer came two days later when President Nixon went on television to address the nation. He sat at his desk with an American flag to his right and a framed photograph of his daughter's wedding visible behind him. As always, he wore a small flag pin on his lapel. He read in a firm, calm voice from the script he held in his hands.

Until March of this year, I remained convinced that the denials were true and that the charges of involvement by members of the White House Staff were false. The comments I made during this period, and the comments made by my Press Secretary in my behalf, were based on the information provided to us at the time we made

those comments. However, new information
then came to me which persuaded me that there
was a real possibility that some of these charges
were true, and suggesting further that there had
been an effort to conceal the facts both from the
public, from you, and from me.

. . . Today, in one of the most difficult decisions of my Presidency, I accepted the resignations of two of my closest associates in the White
House—Bob Haldeman, John Ehrlichman—
two of the finest public servants it has been my
privilege to know.

Nixon then announced that he was naming a new
attorney general and that his counsel, John Dean, had also
resigned. In reality, Nixon had fired Dean. Dash described
the president's announcement as a "volcanic explosion."[55]
Nixon had accepted the resignations of his top aides and
of his attorney general and fired his lawyer. The Watergate
scandal had forced most of the president's highest-level
staff to leave the White House. Nothing like it had ever
happened before.

Dash realized that the people who had left the Nixon
administration were probably the people with the answers
the Senate committee was after. The answers the public

needed to hear. But even if the grand jury charged any of them with crimes, they wouldn't go to trial for months yet. How would the public know what to think or whom to trust in the meantime? The Senate committee had to "set the record straight—to put the witnesses in public hearings to tell the Watergate story to the whole country, not from rumors or anonymous sources, but as . . . eyewitnesses to the facts."[56]

The Senate Watergate Committee owed it to the American people to hold its hearings on national television where everyone could see and hear them. But would anyone care? Would they bother to watch? Dash thought they would.

Sam Dash believed that John Dean was the Senate committee's best chance to get to the facts. Dean had been close to the president and had admitted that he'd broken the law and knew he'd pay a price for that. He wanted to talk. Dash needed to find out what Dean had to say and whether he could be believed. He met Dean and Dean's lawyer late on a Saturday afternoon, expecting John Dean to be like most of the other White House men he'd talked to—ready to say anything or accuse anyone. They hadn't been interested in telling the truth, certainly not the whole truth—they just wanted to keep themselves out of prison.

But after listening to Dean for a time, he decided Dean wasn't like that.

Dash started by asking Dean what he knew about the Watergate break-in, but Dean cut him off before he could finish his first question. "Sam, that is not the beginning," he said impatiently. The Watergate burglary was only one of many such acts and wasn't unusual. He went on:

> When I've told you everything, you will see that a way of life had developed in the White House which made a burglary . . . almost normal behavior . . . It's worse than anything you can imagine.[57]

Dean said that he had stolen some documents from the White House right before he was fired and had given them to Judge Sirica. He claimed that they proved that a year before the break-in, in 1971, President Richard Nixon had approved a plan for using police-state, strongman tactics in the United States—wiretapping, bugging, stealing, breaking and entering, anything and everything—against law-abiding Americans.

Dash had started talking with Dean at five in the afternoon. Before he realized it, it was two in the morning.

Nine hours and Dean had hardly scratched the surface of what he wanted to say. They met again the next night, Sunday. The volume and ugliness of Dean's information was overwhelming.

Dash described his meetings to Senator Sam Ervin, the chair of the Senate Watergate Committee. Ervin listened, his face growing red.

> If Dean is telling the truth, then we've come mighty close to losing the Constitution . . . and the kind of country it has nurtured. . . . With all their [the president's men] patriotic talk . . . they have represented the most dangerous subversive threat to American ideals and government. We've got to awaken the American people to this danger . . . [58]

Dash agreed. The public hearings had to be done right. He again met with Dean and listened for hours more. If even a third of what Dean told him was true, he thought, it would mean the end of Richard Nixon's presidency.

Long after midnight, Dash got into his car and started home. The streets were nearly empty, the houses dark. Most people were asleep in their beds, unaware of what Dash now knew. The truth of the situation washed over him. People had to understand what the president had done and was still doing. That's what the first words of the Constitution—*We the People*—were all about. But Dash's responsibility as chief counsel was terrible. He was going to present "evidence that would show the American people that their president was a criminal."

There, in the middle of the night, exhausted and devastated by Dean's story, Sam Dash started to cry.[59]

CHAPTER 8

Revelations

MAY–JULY 1973

S enator Sam Ervin of North Carolina entered the Senate Caucus Room—a marble-columned, high-ceilinged space famous for the historic hearings held there—as cameras flashed and clicked, reporters jostled for position, and television cameras whirred. Even the air seemed full of anticipation and tension. Ervin saw the televised hearings as a chance to get to the bottom of Watergate and give the nation a huge civics lesson at the same time. People needed to see what the committee was doing and why. He was eager to get the televised hearings underway on this beautiful morning—May 17, 1973.

The seven committee members, four Democrats and three Republicans, took their seats at the polished mahogany desk that stretched across the front of the room. Their aides sat behind them ready to provide documents and legal memos. As chairman of the committee, Senator Ervin had the center seat.

Senators Howard Baker (left) and Sam Ervin listen to testimony during the Senate Watergate Committee hearings.

Ervin sounded like the small-town, Southern native that he was. He'd been in the Senate for nearly twenty years but still liked to call himself "a simple country lawyer." People who knew him generally laughed when he said that. They were aware that he'd graduated from Harvard Law with honors. They didn't laugh, however, when the senator talked about the US Constitution. Ervin had a reputation as a constitutional expert.

The room fell silent when the senator leaned into a microphone and began to speak. His hands shook a little, but he wasn't nervous. It was just age. Pieces of his thinning white hair floated around his head like tiny clouds, and the lines in his heavy face showed a man who smiled often. He was not smiling today.

> We are beginning these hearings today in an atmosphere of utmost gravity. The questions that have been raised in the wake of the June 17th break-in strike at the very undergirding [foundation] of our democracy. If the many allegations [accusations] made to this date are true, then the burglars who broke into the headquarters of the Democratic National Committee at the Watergate were in effect breaking into the home of every citizen of the United States.
>
> If these allegations prove to be true, what they were seeking to steal was not the jewels, money, or other property of American citizens, but something much more valuable—their most precious heritage, the right to vote in a free election.

Those were powerful words. Did the people watching really appreciate the importance of voting in free elections?

Television in 1973 consisted of three major networks—NBC, ABC, and CBS—and a couple of new kinds of networks such as PBS—Public Broadcasting Service—best known then for *Sesame Street*. There were no cable networks like Nickelodeon or Disney. There was no such thing as streaming on Amazon or Netflix. It was important to the committee, therefore, that the major networks show the hearings. By law, networks at that time had to present both sides of political issues, and after the first week of testimony they agreed to take turns, rotating with one network airing the hearings one day and another the next. None of the three networks wanted to lose their daytime audiences entirely by canceling regular shows too often. Only PBS showed every minute every day, "gavel to gavel," and then repeated the broadcast each evening.

On day two of the hearings, James McCord—the Watergate burglar who'd written to Judge Sirica after the trial—told the committee that a Nixon aide had promised him *executive clemency* if he refused to talk during and after the trial. In other words, the president would pardon him and he wouldn't go to prison no matter what the judge and jury decided.

Whoa. How can the judge and jury not matter?

The US Constitution gives the president the "power to grant reprieves and pardons for offenses against the United States. . . ." That means that the president can set aside or wipe away the legal consequences of a conviction against anyone in a federal case. (The president cannot set aside convictions in state courts—that's a state governor's power.)

The power to pardon provides a way to ensure justice if someone is convicted but that conviction turns out to be a mistake. A presidential pardon can free the wrongfully convicted and wipe their record clean. In other cases, a person might be pardoned in exchange for information about more serious crimes or about more dangerous criminals. Occasionally, a president pardons someone for personal reasons, though most experts agree that that is not what the framers intended.

McCord's testimony pushed journalists to wonder if Richard Nixon himself could be connected to Watergate. Why else would he be willing to grant James McCord a pardon for not talking during and after the trial? The public had the same question, and more people tuned in to watch. They were especially anxious to see John Dean's testimony. Americans knew Dean's name by then. He'd been in the headlines since February, two months before his firing in late April.

Dean, however, had asked for time to get all his thoughts written down. He hadn't kept a diary or journal when he worked in the White House and couldn't get to his appointments and meetings calendars once he was fired. So almost everything he said had to come from memory and piecing things together. It would take time to reconstruct the whole story, but he admitted that he'd been in on the illegal Watergate cover-up from the start and knew more than almost anyone about what had happened and why. Dash scheduled Dean to begin his testimony before the committee on June 25, about a month after the beginning of the hearings.

The White House used the time to throw doubt on Dean's honesty as a witness. Aides said he had made false accusations to the prosecutors and would do so again with the Senate committee. He would lie to save himself and would lie about a number of White House aides. The attacks were effective. Many Americans wondered if they should believe whatever Dean said before the committee. Some strong Nixon supporters wrote letters expressing their anger at Dean's disloyalty to the president. And a few days before Dean was set to testify, Sam Dash received an unsigned note printed in big capital letters:

JOHN DEAN WILL NEVER TESTIFY.
HE WILL BE DEAD.

US marshals went to Dean's house in Alexandria, Virginia, just across the Potomac River from Washington. One of them stayed inside the house while the others kept watch outside. More marshals would bring Dean and his wife to the hearing room each morning and take them home at night. Two marshals planned to sit behind Dean during the testimony while police guarded every door. Sam Dash wondered how Watergate could get any more serious.[60]

The Caucus Room filled to overflowing on June 25. Rows of spectators stood behind the last seats. Far more reporters than usual crowded around the assigned tables. And all three networks canceled their regular programming to broadcast Dean's testimony.

John Dean was a slight, balding young man in his mid-thirties with horn-rimmed glasses and serious eyes. He entered the room surrounded by US marshals and Capitol police guards. The security increased viewers' feelings that they were watching something very important.

Millions of Americans watched former White House Counsel John Dean's testimony before the Senate Watergate Committee.

Dean stood with his right hand raised and swore that he would tell the truth. Most people thought he looked smart and studious, like a young man who could go far in his career. He didn't come across the way they imagined a criminal would, even though he had admitted breaking the law. He sat and began reading the statement he'd prepared.

He spoke in a monotone with no expression, later explaining that he didn't want to sound dramatic. No one in the Caucus Room even whispered—Dean's words created a sense of drama no matter how flat his tone was. He continued reading for an hour and then another hour and still no one moved. Across the country, people paused in their work and gathered in front of televisions in restaurants, offices, and homes. Dean kept reading, building a "mountain of facts."[61] He read for over six hours—some 60,000 words, 245 pages in length.

The next morning, John Dean began answering the committee's questions. Americans in record numbers tuned in again. Some brought tiny portable televisions to their workplaces. Others gathered in stores that sold televisions so they could watch at least some of the testimony. Many who couldn't get to a television or radio called friends or relatives every hour or two to get a summary of the hearing. Most cab drivers set their radios on the hearing, and customers asked those who didn't to turn it on. Some people at airports got so interested in Dean's testimony that they missed their flights, while other passengers chose to keep watching rather than board their planes.

Sam Dash felt relief. The American people *did* care, so much so that television networks saw their ratings go up.

During his five days of testimony, Dean described a

long list of illegal and unethical activities that he said were commonplace at the White House. He admitted that he'd done illegal and unethical things himself early in the cover-up. In fact, he was the one who organized it and oversaw the bribery payments. In March 1973, he met with President Nixon and told him there were problems. "There is a cancer on the presidency," Dean said. It had to be cut out or it would take them all down, even the president. The meeting with the president went on for nearly two hours. Toward the end, Dean discussed the specific dangers to all of the White House men involved in the cover-up, including the president. Then he said, "There's the problem of the continued blackmail. It'll cost money."

According to Dean, Nixon asked, "How much money do you need?" When Dean answered, the president responded, "You could get a million dollars. And you could get it in cash. I know where it could be gotten."

After that meeting, Dean said, he realized that Richard Nixon wasn't going to come clean or tell his people to be truthful. John Dean decided he had to go to the investigators himself and tell them what he knew, admitting his own guilt. But he had no intention of taking all the blame alone while Haldeman and Ehrlichman and the others got away with what they'd done.

Americans were stunned. Dean was believable—70

percent of people who watched or listened said they thought he was telling the truth—but it wasn't a truth they liked hearing.[62]

Senator Howard Baker, a Republican from Tennessee and a member of the Senate Watergate Committee, questioned Dean on the fifth and last day of his testimony. Baker had supported Richard Nixon for years. In his campaign for a second term in the Senate, Baker used the phrase "a close friend and trusted advisor of our President, Richard M. Nixon."[63] He'd maintained his loyalty to the president and defended him from the start of the Watergate scandal, believing that the Democrats were using the Watergate break-in as a political weapon to defeat Richard Nixon.

Baker had argued for limited hearings with limited witnesses. He'd met with Nixon and told him he would make sure the committee treated him fairly. He'd even given the White House information he shouldn't have revealed. But as he listened to John Dean's testimony, he wavered. Like many Americans, Baker hoped that the president's men had shielded Nixon from what they were doing. Surely, the president didn't know about all the dirty tricks and the planned break-in ahead of time. Surely, he hadn't tried to cover anything up or known that his aides were doing that.

Senator Baker wanted to make it clear that Richard Nixon was innocent in the midst of so many accusations and so much complicated information. The president's aides, including John Dean, had made terrible mistakes, but . . .

Baker pressed Dean on his testimony, trying to show that there was no firsthand or direct evidence that the president had done anything wrong. He said, "My primary thesis [point] is, what did the president know, and when did he know it?" He wanted an exact answer from Dean. He wanted Dean to say that the president hadn't known much and only found out what his aides had done in March 1973, as he claimed.

Dean didn't do what Baker hoped he would. Instead, he told Baker, the committee, and the public that he and Nixon had discussed the break-in, the cover-up, the bribes, and more at least thirty-five different times in the last year, starting in September 1972. Baker's confidence in Richard Nixon cracked. But he had a choice. He could continue to find ways to defend the president. Or he could work to find the truth. It wasn't an easy decision.

Two weeks later, after hearing additional witnesses, the committee called Alexander Butterfield to testify. Few people knew Butterfield's name. He hadn't been in the news and didn't know nearly as much as other witnesses did about the Watergate break-in or the cover-up. He'd been Nixon's deputy chief of staff but left that job at the end of the president's first term. Now he was in front of the committee because Sam Dash had sent his team searching for someone with the answer to a huge question.

John Dean had testified that one time when he was talking with the president, he had the feeling that there might be a recording device in the room. The committee needed to know if that was true. It could change everything.

Dash's team had mapped the White House offices to figure out who sat where and who worked for whom. They knew that Alexander Butterfield used to have a desk just outside the door to the Oval Office. They brought him in for questioning on a Friday afternoon while Dash was in the Caucus Room.

Eager to get home for a special Sabbath dinner and his wedding anniversary, Dash was on his way out the door earlier than usual when his phone rang. One of the lawyers who questioned Butterfield had to see him right away. No, it couldn't wait for Monday.

Dash listened as his assistants described what Butterfield had told them. Then he called Sam Ervin and gave him the news. Ervin drawled his amazement. "That is the most remarkable discovery of evidence I have learned about in my entire experience in the practice of the law as a judge on the bench and as a United States senator."[64]

Butterfield wasn't happy about being called to testify and wanted to avoid it. Nixon didn't want him to testify either. He claimed that the Constitution's separation of powers allowed the president to refuse all requests from the Senate, including testimony from people who worked in the executive branch.

Sam Ervin disagreed. The committee issued a *subpoena* (order) to Butterfield on Monday morning, but he still resisted. Finally, Senator Ervin threatened to have the sergeant-at-arms, the chief law enforcement officer and head of security for the Senate, come arrest him. At that point, Butterfield agreed to appear.

Butterfield's testimony was brief. Within minutes, the important question came from one of the lawyers for the committee. "Mr. Butterfield, are you aware of any listening devices in the office of the president?"

Butterfield paused for a full five seconds. Finally, he said, "I was aware of listening devices, yes sir."

People watching at home or at work heard the gasps in the Caucus Room. Recordings. *Tapes.* There was a tape recorder in the Oval Office. According to Butterfield, everyone and every conversation that took place in the Oval Office was recorded. Who had ordered such a thing? President Richard Nixon.

Senator Howard Baker knew what Butterfield was going to say before he said it. He had the same information Dash and Ervin did—he'd talked to Butterfield himself. But hearing it out loud and hearing the reactions of the spectators and reporters made it worse. Baker sat next to Sam Ervin at the huge desk with his chin in his hand, his eyes cast down, his face gray.

Howard Baker had made his decision. He knew he'd hear criticism from some Republicans and might anger the people who had elected him. But it didn't matter. He decided to go after the facts, questioning witnesses like a good prosecutor, and pushing them to tell the whole truth no matter how painful it was. His deepest loyalty was not to the president, but to the country and the Constitution.

Newspapers and television newscasts made Butterfield's revelation of the tapes the top story all over the country that night and the next day. The *Washington Post* printed five tapes-related stories just on page one of the July 17 paper. Many cabinet heads and administration officials told reporters they were stunned, incredulous, astonished. Readers wondered if it was even legal to record people without their knowledge.

Sam Dash's team didn't care about the legality just then. That could wait. What they cared about now was that a lot of the testimony of the last weeks could be checked. Most important, the tapes could prove one way or the other the truth of John Dean's devastating "mountain of facts." As one article said, the tapes were the "ultimate witness."[65]

But how could they get Richard Nixon to give them his Oval Office recordings?

Some 85 percent of American adults watched at least parts of the Senate Watergate hearings. They watched witness after witness and didn't like how often some former White House aides, Bob Haldeman in particular, said "I don't remember" or "I can't recall." Viewers doubted those witnesses were being honest or telling the *whole* truth as they had sworn to do. They found other witnesses like John Dean and Alexander Butterfield sympathetic and gasped at their revelations along with the spectators in the Caucus Room. But the star of the hearings, in most Americans' opinion, was committee chairman Senator Sam Ervin.

The "simple country lawyer" with his deep Southern accent and quirky charm was made for television—one journalist said Ervin had a "face like a giant friendly turnip."[66] The senator from North Carolina sometimes got his point across by quoting Shakespeare. Other times, he used passages from the Bible. Viewers liked his country sayings. They admired his knowledge of the Constitution. They appreciated his clear explanations of difficult ideas. And they couldn't look away from his eyebrows.

Ervin's eyebrows had a life of their own. They stood out thick and dark against his thin, white hair and framed his piercing eyes. The brows came together when Ervin was angry, crawled up his forehead when he doubted what a witness was saying, and wriggled like nervous caterpillars when he was thinking hard. Simply put, Sam Ervin was entertaining to watch. That helped him as he subtly taught Americans how their nation's government worked.

People all over the country pulled out old schoolbooks or used their children's textbooks to look up long-forgotten details of civics classes. What checks does the legislative branch have on the executive branch? Do White House aides work for the president himself or for the government? Do they work for the American people the way the FBI is supposed to? What role do the courts play in all this? It seemed the Constitution wasn't as long or as complicated as a lot of people thought—really just a few pages. Manageable.

Many Americans would have been dismayed if they'd known about Senator Ervin's support of segregation and the Vietnam War, though his ideas weren't unusual in the early 1970s. Many people who did know his positions on

Senator Sam Ervin became a folk hero to many Americans during the Senate Watergate hearings.

those enormous issues disagreed with him wholeheart-edly. Most people, though, didn't keep up with the views of senators outside their own states. And as the Watergate hearings went on, more and more Americans saw Sam Ervin as a hero of sorts. They sent telegrams and letters thanking him for the hearings, and they rooted for him as he questioned key witnesses. A man in California even started a Sam Ervin fan club.

Ervin, a Democrat, had begun the Senate investigation believing that Richard Nixon's aides committed crimes out of too much enthusiasm for getting their boss reelected. Like Republican Senator Baker, he couldn't imagine that Nixon himself was involved. Surely, the president's men had protected him from what they were doing. But the testimony Ervin heard during the early investigation, the calls and meetings he had with Sam Dash, and now the hearings, led him in another direction. He had little patience for the kind of thinking that allowed a president to trample on the Constitution.

John Ehrlichman was Nixon's number two aide before resigning in late April. During his questioning by the committee, he argued with Ervin and other members. He challenged them on details and the meaning of what he'd said or done or what the president had done. Ehrlichman had a habit of lifting one eyebrow and curling his lip in what most people would call a sneer. Sam Ervin found him arrogant.[67]

Ehrlichman testified in late July and faced questions about the illegal activities that occurred long before the Watergate break-in. He insisted that the break-in at Daniel Ellsberg's doctor's office in 1971 was perfectly legal. The president had the power to order such a break-in, he argued. Ervin challenged him, glaring over his reading glasses as his eyebrows flew up and down. He quoted the Fourth Amendment and bellowed that *no* president has the power to ignore the Constitution's basic protection against unreasonable searches of Americans' private property.

Ehrlichman and his lawyer still argued. A law passed in the 1960s gave the president that power, they said. If foreign intelligence activities—spying—threatened the nation's security, the president could order a break-in. The law said so. Ellsberg might have been sending information to Russia.

Ervin leaned forward in his chair and reminded Ehrlichman that he, Ervin, had helped write that very law. He waved a copy of the law in the air and thrust a gnarled finger at Ehrlichman. Getting louder by the minute, he nearly yelled, "Foreign intelligence activities had nothin' to do with" the opinion of Ellsberg's doctor. Doctors' records and foreign spying were not related.

"How do you know that, Mr. Chairman?" Ehrlichman responded curtly.

Ervin threw his head up and shouted, "Because I can understand the English language as my mother taught!"

The Caucus Room erupted in laughter and applause. The senator banged his gavel several times, but the laughter and clapping went on. Even John Ehrlichman smiled. He was no match for the chairman. The tension broke.

In the meantime, tension behind the scenes increased. It had been almost two weeks since Butterfield's statement about the tapes, but the Senate committee hadn't seen a single one of those recordings. If the president continued to refuse their requests as he'd refused other requests for documents, they could issue a subpoena. But if he defied that, what more could they do? What would happen next?

CHAPTER 9

Prosecuting the President's Men

MAY–OCTOBER 1973

By the early summer of 1973, Richard Nixon was in trouble. He'd built a barricade of lies, bribes, and threats to protect himself and his plans. But that barricade wasn't as strong as he and his men wanted it to be. First, while their lies about the news media had turned a number of Americans against the nation's major newspapers and news programs, they hadn't done enough. Nixon had told his people, "You must keep up the attack on the media. You've got to keep destroying their credibility."[68] From the start, Woodward and Bernstein's efforts had kept the story alive and in front of Congress as well as the public. Nixon hadn't been able to stop them. Instead, the *Washington Post*, the *New York Times*, and now other papers and magazines, as well as the network television newscasts, kept reporting one shocking story after another. The First Amendment held.

Second, the president and his aides had bribed the Watergate burglars and their handlers and made vague

Department of Justice Headquarters in Washington, DC

threats to keep them from telling the truth in front of the grand jury or at their trials. They'd worked to limit the FBI's investigation as well. Those tactics had worked for a while. But when Judge John Sirica spoke out publicly and said that the trial had not produced all the facts in the case, James McCord had dared step forward with the truth in spite of threats and bribery.

Third, there was the grand jury that had indicted the Watergate burglars back in September and was still listening to evidence in other areas of the Watergate case in early 1973. That grand jury could indict more people—people connected to the cover-up and the secret fund and all the rest—and there was nothing Nixon could do to stop it even as the indictments got closer and closer to the Oval Office. Only the judicial branch of government can dismiss a grand jury, and Judge John Sirica had no intention of doing so. There was no telling how many more trials would come out of it.

And naturally, Nixon had hoped that Republicans in the Senate would vote against creating a committee to do its own Watergate investigation. They didn't. The vote to establish the Senate Watergate Committee had been unanimous. It was one more crack in the barricade. But the president believed that he would at least get support from the Republicans on the committee. Surely, they would protect him. At first, Howard Baker had given the president reason to think that would be the case even though Connecticut Republican Lowell Weicker was annoyingly independent and asked a lot of tough questions. But Baker let Nixon down when he rethought his loyalties in the face of the evidence. The president hadn't been able to control the legislative branch after all. The best he could do was to refuse to give the committee any documents that might help them.

That left Richard Nixon with few options. How would the barricade hold? How would he keep his secrets hidden?

Some members of the Senate had talked about appointing a special prosecutor. His job would be to investigate Watergate without White House influence. Nixon had resisted the idea. It seemed safer to have the prosecutors already in the Department of Justice simply continue the investigation they had started. In late April, though, shortly before his top aides resigned and the Senate committee began its hearings, the president thought about the idea again. The *right kind* of special prosecutor might help him repair and build up his barricade.

What makes a prosecutor special?

Prosecutors are government lawyers. They investigate crimes and then present the evidence during the trial. Federal prosecutors in the United States are part of the Department of Justice in the executive branch of government. Some cases present challenges to federal prosecutors. Perhaps the accused person is a high-level government official in the executive branch. Perhaps that person has close connections to the president or the attorney general—the prosecutors' bosses. This kind of awkward situation is called a *conflict of interest*. In such cases, the attorney general may appoint a special prosecutor—an experienced lawyer who does not work for the government and is known for being fair. This special prosecutor then works for the government temporarily to investigate and prosecute the case and any related crimes such as perjury. Special prosecutors have more independence from the Justice Department and executive branch than regular federal prosecutors.

Nixon suggested to Chief of Staff Bob Haldeman that the attorney general could appoint a special prosecutor for the Watergate case. That person would make sure that all the "right" people were indicted and that certain other people were not indicted. Then he could tell the public that everyone involved in the case who *should* be accused of a crime *was* accused of a crime. He could say it was time to stop investigating.

Haldeman liked the idea. He understood that Nixon

wanted a special prosecutor for show. Someone who could convince the country that the investigation was thorough and complete but who would not really go after all the facts. Perfect.

The same week, Nixon appointed Elliot Richardson as his new attorney general. Richardson had worked for Richard Nixon since the beginning of the president's first term. He'd served in two cabinet positions. Everyone agreed that Richardson was brilliant and hardworking. But not everyone was sure of his principles or values. Nixon knew that Richardson was very ambitious, perhaps ambitious enough to do whatever the president asked in order to keep moving up in government. Richardson had also been very loyal to the president, and the president hoped that that loyalty was Richardson's key principle and highest value. Especially when it came to appointing a special prosecutor. But he didn't fully explain his idea to Elliot Richardson. He assumed Richardson would already know what kind of special prosecutor he wanted.

Richardson had to meet with the Senate Judiciary Committee and answer their questions before they would vote to approve his nomination. He told them that he planned to appoint a special prosecutor for Watergate. The committee members insisted that whoever he chose had to be independent of the attorney general and the president. That wasn't what Richardson planned. But he realized that if he wanted to become attorney general, he would have to agree to the committee's demand. And he would have to choose someone acceptable to both Democrats and Republicans in the Senate.

The new attorney general called Archibald Cox in mid-May, just as the Senate's televised hearings started. Cox had taught Elliot Richardson at Harvard Law School many years earlier. But he was surprised that Richardson wanted *him* to be the Watergate special prosecutor. Richardson didn't tell Cox that four other lawyers had said no to the job.[69]

Archibald Cox, Archie to his friends, was the kind of man Richard Nixon liked to dislike. He'd grown up in a privileged family while Nixon was poor. The oldest of seven children, he had a childhood filled with opportunities while Nixon's early life was cold and tragic. Cox had always been athletic. Nixon was not. And when Cox got into Harvard, there was no doubt he could go there. But Richardson knew Cox as a recognized expert on constitutional law who had worked as a trial lawyer and as a government lawyer, as well as a law professor. His students and people who worked for him claimed that he made ridiculously difficult demands of them. He did, but Cox

Archibald Cox, an expert on constitutional law, served as Watergate special prosecutor, May-October 1973.

put the same kinds of demands on himself, often rewriting legal papers again and again until he was certain his work could not be better. No one doubted Cox's fairness and honesty, and Richardson knew that both Republicans and

Democrats in Congress respected him. Not knowing that the president wanted a puppet special prosecutor, someone he could control, Richardson appointed Cox without asking for Nixon's opinion. The president was shocked and angry. But it was too late. Nixon had to pretend that Cox had his full support—if he didn't at least pretend, people would think he had something to hide.[70]

Tall, thin, and fit at sixty-one, Cox kept his hair in a crew cut and always wore a bow tie no matter what the current fashion was. He knew he was smart and liked challenges. Later, he said that he thought the job of Special Watergate Prosecutor would be "fun."[71]

Cox hired the best lawyers he could find for his staff, each with the knowledge and skills he needed. He divided the investigation into several categories of crimes. Then he assigned a team of investigators and lawyers to each category. First came the break-in and cover-up. Yes, federal prosecutors had investigated and tried the burglary case. But they hadn't prosecuted anyone for the planning, financing, or cover-up. Like FBI investigators, they'd been told to stick with the burglary and go no further. So Cox planned to have one team look at all the information again in order to get at the questions the original investigation didn't ask. In legal terms a cover-up is called *obstruction of justice.* It's a very serious crime. And new details of that obstruction seemed to ooze out of the White House and into the newspapers every day.

A second team was assigned to Nixon's secret security group, which called itself "the Plumbers." The Plumbers were responsible for the doctor's office break-in, the wiretapping, the bugging, and other spying crimes. Cox had a third team dig into the money behind the Watergate break-in. That money trail led to a huge volume of evidence showing that the Nixon people had violated campaign finance laws over and over again. Another team took the business bribery cases. And a final team investigated the "dirty tricks" campaign that had seriously harmed the Democratic primaries.

The task was gigantic. Like Sam Dash at the Senate committee, Cox hired nearly a hundred people—lawyers, trial experts, prosecutors, investigators, and a crowd of young graduates with limitless energy. They took office space a few blocks from the White House on K Street, and Cox insisted that it had to be as secure as the most secure office at the FBI.[72]

The team worked twelve hours a day, sometimes seven days a week. Cox generally took time on Sundays to walk around the city or drive out to the Blue Ridge Mountains and hike the peaceful trails of Shenandoah National Park.

He liked to get the exercise and clear his mind before starting another grueling week. No one got much rest any other time.

Hold on. Why were there so many investigations?

The FBI is part of the Justice Department in the executive branch. It conducted the first Watergate investigation beginning the night of the break-in in June 1972. FBI agents interviewed hundreds of people and collected thousands of pages of evidence. But they had instructions to investigate the burglars and the break-in only and not follow up on other possible crimes. Their evidence went to the Justice Department prosecutors. The prosecutors presented it to the grand jury. The grand jury would decide who should go to trial for specific crimes.

The special prosecutor went to work in May 1973. He led the second criminal investigation. The attorney general had appointed a special prosecutor because many people criticized the Justice Department investigation. They thought it had not gone far enough. And the president wanted a special prosecutor because he thought he could control that prosecutor's investigation. The special prosecutor's evidence also went to a grand jury.

The Senate Watergate Committee's investigation was part of Congress's check on the executive branch. The Senate had a duty to inform the public about executive branch misdeeds. The Watergate Committee was also responsible for suggesting new laws that could prevent any similar scandals in the future.

The Senate and special prosecutor investigations went on at the same time. But each had its own job to do under the Constitution. They listened to many of the same witnesses and asked similar questions. The Senate held its hearings publicly, but the special prosecutor's evidence was kept secret. By law, evidence presented to a grand jury is not open to the public.

By mid-July, the lawyers working for Cox had made progress in several areas. But the president and his lawyer refused to give them any cooperation. For example, they asked Cox to make his requests for documents very specific so the White House could decide whether to turn them over or not. But how was Cox supposed to know what to ask for when he'd never seen any documents at all? Cox and his assistants debated what to do.

Then, in the middle of July, a group of young lawyers on the team stood around a small television. The Senate hearings were on and the staffers couldn't resist watching for just a few minutes. That's when Alexander Butterfield sat down to testify and told the committee about the recording devices in the Oval Office.

"Can you *believe* that? Can you *believe* that?" shouted one young lawyer, stunned at what he'd heard.

Cox wanted those tapes. He needed them. Could he be specific about which ones he wanted? The team had Haldeman's and Ehrlichman's office diaries showing the meetings they had with the president. If Cox could get the tapes from those days, specific tapes from specific days, it could break the case open. But asking for the tapes presented real risks. Nixon wouldn't just turn them over. Cox could subpoena the tapes. But if Nixon defied the subpoena, the case was likely to go all the way to the Supreme Court. There was no telling what the justices would say—Nixon had appointed four of the nine members of the Supreme Court himself.

Whatever the odds were, Cox decided to take the risk. He'd promised to follow the evidence, and the tapes were probably the biggest batch of evidence he'd ever have. Archibald Cox had spent thirty-five years studying legal arguments, developing legal arguments, and teaching student lawyers how to analyze and write legal arguments. Now he needed the most persuasive legal writing possible. He turned to two team attorneys. "Let's get started."[73] He was about to issue a subpoena to the president of the United States.

In the meantime, Sam Ervin and Sam Dash faced the same dilemma. Sure, Ervin had threatened to send the Senate's sergeant-at-arms to arrest Butterfield if he refused to come before the committee. But the senator couldn't imagine doing that with the president of the United States. He couldn't have the sergeant-at-arms go to the White House with handcuffs ready for the president. It would look like the legislature was overthrowing the executive. Like a coup or a revolution of some kind.

A week before anyone knew about the tapes, Nixon had refused to give the committee the documents they asked for—memos and meeting notes that might shed light on the accusations of a cover-up. Ervin had called the president, hoping to set up a meeting to discuss the situation. But Nixon didn't listen to anything the senator said. He sounded angry and repeated over and over, "You're out to get me, you're out to get me."[74] Ervin found the conversation unsettling. He'd wondered if Nixon was well.

Now the issue was the tapes. Ervin knew Nixon's argument. The president believed he had "absolute, unreviewable power, and was not subject to the process of any court."[75] Nixon's argument wasn't new—other presidents had claimed *executive privilege* too. But Richard Nixon was taking the idea to a new level, what Ervin described as "way outside the atmosphere."[76]

What? Regular Americans can't ignore a subpoena. Can the president?

That depends. The Constitution does not mention executive privilege or even the idea of it. But presidents say that keeping conversations and documents private is part of the separation of powers. If they can't protect their conversations, they say, their aides and advisors will not speak freely and openly and presidents won't get the advice they need.

Congress often argues that the public has the right to know what the president is doing. But both sides agree that some conversations and documents must stay private—war plans, discussions of new weapons, information on American spies. All sorts of secret things need to stay that way to protect the country and individual Americans.

The first president to argue for the idea of executive privilege was George Washington, but no one called it that until the 1950s. Most of the time when Congress wants documents or testimony from the White House and the White House resists, one side or the other gives in. In George Washington's case, he ended up giving Congress the requested papers.

Ervin knew history and the Constitution very well. He agreed that presidents did have executive privilege, but not the kind Nixon claimed. Ervin argued that the president had the power to keep communications secret only when he was doing his official duties. That power did not apply to "illegal or unethical or political activities." And it did not allow any president to withhold material that dealt with crimes under investigation. Ervin said that wasn't executive privilege at all. It was "nothing but *executive poppycock.*"[77] And if Nixon did withhold that kind of material, it would put the president above the Constitution.[78]

A week after Butterfield's bombshell, both Senator Sam Ervin and Special Prosecutor Archibald Cox issued subpoenas for the White House tapes. They knew Nixon

The subpoena commanding Richard Nixon to provide evidence to the court

would refuse and they'd have to go to court. They knew the battle would be ugly, but they believed in one of the great principles of democracy—no person is above the law. Not even the president.

CHAPTER 10

Turning Point

AUGUST–OCTOBER 1973

S pecial Prosecutor Archibald Cox didn't know what the tapes would or would not prove. He didn't know if they would help or hurt Richard Nixon. But he had studied everything there was to study on whether the president should have to turn them over or not. He'd concluded that he should.

Cox and several assistants spent over three weeks reviewing every law book anywhere that mentioned executive power. They read the words of legal scholars as far back as thirteenth-century England. They reviewed cases from Thomas Jefferson's presidency in the early 1800s and Harry Truman's in the 1940s and 1950s. They wrote, revised, and wrote again. They argued over small phrases and single words. By the middle of August, they were as ready as they could be to argue their case in court.

Judge John Sirica had presided over the Watergate case—the whole case, not just the burglary trial—from the beginning. He had signed the subpoena Archibald

Cox issued (a prosecutor must have a judge sign any subpoena before issuing it). Now, on July 26, 1973, he heard the arguments on the president's refusal to obey the subpoena.

Sirica read aloud the letter he had received from President Nixon that morning. The president argued that he, as chief executive, could not demand any specific action from the courts. In turn, the courts could not demand any specific action from the executive. It was part of the separation of powers. Nixon would give the court and the grand jury material he wanted to give them. But the court had no power to make him turn over anything more.

Cox stood and explained why he needed specific tapes and why the president's argument was weak. Grand juries need and are allowed to have the best evidence possible to do their jobs. That had been an accepted rule of law for centuries. Why should the president be an exception to that rule?

The grand jury was in the courtroom to hear the president's letter and Cox's arguments. That was very unusual, but Judge Sirica had wanted the ordinary citizens who made up the grand jury to be there in person. Now he asked them if he should send the president an *order to show cause*. It would demand that the president or his attorney explain to the court why the president did not have to obey the court's subpoena. The grand jury's response was a unanimous yes and Sirica signed the order.

Later, Judge Sirica described that moment when the grand jury demanded that the president follow the same law everyone else did:

> Here was the grand jury made up of ordinary citizens . . . , some of them poor people, telling the president of the United States, the most powerful man in the world, to turn over the tapes. If there ever was a moment that gave meaning to the idea that in our democracy, the people govern themselves, that was it.[79]

In early August the president's lawyer delivered his *brief* or argument. It was thirty-four pages filled with quotations and reminders of earlier, related court cases. Sirica thought the brief was impressive but found its last arguments unconvincing. He wondered how Archibald Cox would respond. A week later, he got his answer, sixty-seven pages with another eighty-five pages of quotations from the witnesses at the Senate hearings.

The following week, the president's lawyer and the special prosecutor met in front of the judge in a courtroom packed with lawyers, other judges, reporters, and anyone else able to get in. A line of people hoping to see some part of the arguments wound down the sidewalk outside and around the corner. This was big. No one had subpoenaed a president since 1807.

The president's lawyer summarized the arguments from his brief and then answered Sirica's questions. Yes, he was sure that the reason the president would not turn over the tapes was that he believed he must protect the privacy of presidential discussions.

Cox then made his arguments, all of them well researched and persuasive. Now it was time to wait for the judge's decision.

John Sirica issued his ruling at the end of August. He had looked for a compromise and ordered the president to give the tapes to him. He would make sure that any parts of the tapes not related to Watergate and anything connected to national security would remain private. But, he said, the decision on what could be kept private belonged to a judge, not the president.[80]

Newscasters announced that Archibald Cox had won and the president would have to turn over the tapes. But Cox and his team knew it wasn't that simple. Sirica hadn't said that Cox would get the tapes. And even if he had, they knew Nixon would appeal the judge's decision. Cox

The Federal Courthouse at Judiciary Square in Washington, DC, is home to the US District Court and the US Court of Appeals for the District of Columbia Circuit.

would have to go to a higher court and present the case again. He and his aides got back to work making their arguments even stronger.

A higher court?
How many kinds of courts are there?

Quite a few. First, each state has its own court system and the federal government has a court system. The Watergate case went through the federal court system only. There are several different kinds of federal courts that handle different kinds of legal matters.

One type of federal court is the US District Court. District courts are sometimes called trial courts, and they are where federal trials take place. District judges such as John Sirica preside over cases, and federal juries decide the outcomes of those cases. There are ninety-four US District Courts with at least one in every state and in the District of Columbia (Washington, DC). Judges in district courts have responsibilities beyond trials. They sign subpoenas, hear arguments as Judge Sirica did with the tapes, and preside over many other kinds of hearings. They oversee the court process in a case from beginning to end.

Appeals courts have a different role. There are twelve US Courts of Appeals, also called circuit courts. Courts of appeal do not hold trials and do not have juries. They hear cases in which one side or the other claims that the district court made a mistake. No one can appeal a verdict just because they don't like the jury's decision. There must be an error by the judge, or in the collection of evidence, or in the law itself. Most cases in the appeals court are decided by a three-judge panel.

Finally, there is the Supreme Court of the United States, made up of a chief justice and eight associate justices. But that can wait.

August had been a rough month for the president. First, there was Cox arguing in court to get the tapes. And arguing very persuasively at that. Then the *Washington Post* reported that Nixon was mistaken when he admitted spending $25,000 of taxpayer money on his homes in California and Florida. He'd actually spent seventeen *million* tax dollars on his personal property. Not long after that, the *Wall Street Journal* exposed a bribery investigation of Nixon's vice president, Spiro Agnew. Agnew was accused of accepting bribes in his White House office. Actual cash in unmarked envelopes delivered to the vice president in the building across the lawn from the Oval Office. It was a disaster.

Richard Nixon was furious—furious with the *Washington Post*, furious that Agnew was in trouble, and furious more than anything with Archibald Cox. The president had agreed to a special prosecutor for Watergate in order to shut the thing down. Instead, just as Nixon feared, Cox was making it worse.

Nixon wrote later, "I felt that he was trying to get me personally. I wanted him out."[81] He called Cox a "partisan viper"—a snake who could see only one side of the situation.[82] A typical East Coast, elite school, bow tie–wearing snob. Nixon was not giving up the tapes. No way. Cox had to go.

Two days after Cox's court argument, Nixon spoke to the nation about Watergate for a second time. He politely told Americans that the Senate had every right to investigate charges against a president. But he had to keep the tapes private because making them public would destroy presidential confidentiality forever. Nixon insisted that the tapes would prove he did not know about the break-in ahead of time and that he'd done nothing to cover up his aides' involvement in criminal activities. The content of the tapes would help him, he said. But giving them up would harm the presidency. Americans weren't sure what to think.

Cox and the president's lawyer went to the appeals court. Again, they argued before a packed courtroom. The appeals court told the two sides to spend a week trying to find a compromise solution that would give the special prosecutor the information he needed and also protect the president's confidentiality. Cox was willing to give it a try, but he soon learned that the president's lawyer and aides had no intention of compromising at all. The court would have to decide one way or the other.

In the meantime, the Senate hearings continued. Americans learned that "rivers of cash flowed" from campaign contributors to CRP and then through a series of other officials and organizations. Ultimately, enormous amounts of that money went illegally into safes and secret funds. It paid for espionage and sabotage to hurt Democrats. In just two days, nearly five million dollars went to a reporter who spied on the Democratic nominee and to the dirty tricks group—the people who messed up Democrats' campaigns—as well as to other shady campaign activities. Five thousand dollars in political donations went toward the break-in at Daniel Ellsberg's doctor's office. Tens of thousands more went to pay off the men arrested for the Watergate break-in.[83]

The special prosecutor's team pressed on too, gathering evidence and interviewing witnesses. There were now two grand juries hearing evidence—one for the break-in and cover-up, and another for all the other categories of crimes Watergate had uncovered. Members of the grand jury heard details of the dirty tricks campaign. They saw evidence of illegal campaign contributions from a variety of business owners who wanted favors. They learned that the special prosecutor's office had gathered evidence and planned to charge several men with perjury—lying under oath—including a former attorney general and several White House aides. Other investigations continued as well. Investigations of the Committee to Reelect the President, investigations of some agencies of the federal government,

of the president's friends, and of more and more businesses. Piles of evidence had uncovered an astonishing
number of crimes.

Nixon put the blame for so much bad publicity and
so many accusations on the press and on Archibald Cox.
He couldn't stop the press, at least not yet. But he wasn't
going to put up with Cox much longer. Someone who
worked at the White House told a reporter, "Over here
they talk about how to get Cox all the time."[84] The trouble
was that "getting" Cox wouldn't be easy. He could only be
fired for "extraordinary improprieties"—terrible wrongdoing.

By early October, the Watergate scandal hung like a dark
cloud over the White House. But the president's job—the
real work of being president—doesn't stop for scandals.
On October 6, 1973, Egypt and Syria suddenly attacked
Israel. On October 10, the crisis over bribery accusations
against the vice president resulted in Spiro Agnew's resignation. On October 12, Nixon ordered United States
military aid to Israel while Russia sent help to Egypt and
Syria. A major war between the world's two superpowers—
the US and the USSR (communist Russia or the Soviet
Union)—looked very possible.

That same day, the US Court of Appeals ruled that

Nixon had to give the subpoenaed tapes to Judge Sirica. The judges had ruled that allowing the president to decide on his own what information he would give the court would be "an invitation to refashion [remake] the Constitution."[85] The president had until October 19 to appeal to the Supreme Court.

Archibald Cox knew he was probably going to lose his job. But he still hoped that he and the White House might reach some agreement. As the deadline for appealing to the Supreme Court approached, however, his hopes dimmed.

The president waited until the last minute and then announced that he would not appeal to the Supreme Court. But he wouldn't turn over the tapes, either. He would give the courts and the Senate committee summaries of the recorded conversations and order Archibald Cox to stop using the courts to get other information from the White House. No more subpoenas.

Cox replied that obeying that order would violate his sworn duty as special prosecutor and, therefore, he could not obey it. He also announced that he would speak to the news media the next day. Cox's team, the press, and the public waited anxiously to see what would happen.

. . .

October 20, a Saturday, dawned bright and warm. It felt more like spring than fall. But reporters had no time to enjoy the weather. The president had issued a statement to the morning papers saying that he had to be able to act decisively in dangerous times. Foreign leaders might "be tempted . . . to misread America's unity and resolve in meeting the challenges we confront abroad." Did that mean that it was unpatriotic to ask for the truth about Watergate because there was a war in the Middle East?[86]

Cox didn't think he was unpatriotic at all. But he wasn't comfortable with confronting the president either. He'd been raised to "honor and respect the president," he told his wife. He was sick at the idea of defying the nation's leader.[87] He went to his office and told his staff that they should keep up their work no matter what. They noticed that he'd dressed differently from usual. He was wearing a long, dark tie. Today was too serious for a bow tie's natural good cheer as Cox stood before reporters and television cameras.

He began, "I read in one of the newspapers this morning the headline 'Cox Defiant.' I don't *feel* defiant. I'm certainly not out to get the president . . . In the end I decided I had to try to stick by what I thought was right."

Cox went on to explain why he needed the tapes and why it would set a very bad example for the future if he gave in and allowed the president to violate the agreement the attorney general had made in hiring him as special proscecutor. He listed the problems he saw with the president's compromise plan. When he finished, reporters started asking questions. He answered some and politely refused to answer others. Then one reporter said, "How could you expect to succeed in this job?"

"I thought it would be worth a try. I thought it was important. If it could be done, I thought it would help the country."[88]

Attorney General Elliot Richardson got a call to come see the president late that afternoon. He knew what it was about. According to the procedures set up for hiring the special prosecutor, only the attorney general could fire him. The president wanted Richardson to fire Archibald Cox. Richardson had wrestled with the idea all week.

As soon as he entered the Oval Office, Elliot Richardson could see that Richard Nixon was angry. He decided to get the whole thing over with. He told the president that he was offering his resignation as attorney general of the United States.

Nixon knew that was what Richardson planned. But he didn't want to lose him. He appealed to Richardson's sense of duty. The country was on the brink of war in

Attorney General Elliot Richardson resigned rather than break his word and fire the special prosecutor.

the Middle East, he argued. He needed his advisors and department heads with him. It didn't work. Then he said, "Elliot, I'm sorry you choose to put your purely personal commitments ahead of the public interest."

Richardson felt his face flush with anger but answered

as calmly as he could, "Mr. President, it would appear that you and I have a different perception [understanding] of the public interest."[89] Elliot Richardson knew what his principles were and had made up his mind. He would not break his word to the Senate and would not break his word to the special prosecutor. Archibald Cox had done nothing that approached "extraordinary impropriety." Richardson would not fire him.

Nixon called in Richardson's deputy, William Ruckelshaus. He, too, refused to fire the special prosecutor. He, too, resigned. Nixon considered them fired. He'd get whoever was next in line at the Justice Department to get rid of Cox.

At about eight thirty that evening, Carl Feldbaum, a young lawyer from the special prosecutor's office, was just sitting down to dinner with his wife and another of Cox's young lawyers when the phone rang. "Archie's been fired. I'll see you at the office."

Leaving their dinner on the table, the three of them got to K Street in record time and left the car on the sidewalk around the corner. As they entered the almost empty building, they saw the guards watching television. A bulletin had interrupted their program. "The country tonight is in the midst of what may be the most serious constitutional crisis in its history," said an obviously shaken newsman.

The lawyers understood the seriousness of the situation. The president was breaking the system of checks and balances. He had defied the judicial branch by refusing to turn over the tapes after the appeals court ordered him to. Anyone else who did that would be in jail for contempt of court. Now the president had defied the legislative branch by breaking the agreement the attorney general made with the Senate before he appointed Archibald Cox as special prosecutor. Anyone else would be held in contempt of Congress. Richard Nixon had declared by his actions that he, the chief executive, was above the other two branches of government and above the Constitution. Without checks and balances, there was nothing to stop the president from taking total control.

Feldbaum and Phil Bakes, the other lawyer, practically ran to their offices with Feldbaum's wife right behind them. According to the network news, Nixon's chief of staff had ordered the FBI to seal the offices of the special prosecutor—not let anything in or out. The lawyers had to protect their work and their evidence before that happened.

Carl Feldbaum, twenty-nine and a deputy prosecutor on the team, opened his office safe with shaking hands. He took out a brown envelope that held three small tapes of witness interviews and handed it to his wife. She pushed the envelope into her jeans and walked carefully to the elevator.

When the elevator opened again, Feldbaum expected to see his wife coming back upstairs. Instead, several FBI agents stepped off. One was a man he knew. The agent had worked with the lawyers on pieces of the investigation and they'd been friendly. "I didn't want to come down here," Agent Angelo Lano said, looking miserable.

The other young lawyer, Phil Bakes, was distraught. "What are you doing here? You should leave now. Why don't you leave?" he pressed as both he and Lano fought back tears.

Lano took a breath. "They'd send somebody else," he answered.

Angelo Lano didn't want to seal the offices, but he was under orders. However, he'd told his boss he absolutely would not search anyone going in or out. For the next hour, staffers from the special prosecutor's office went up and down in the elevators, back and forth quietly, saying nothing. Lano and the other FBI agents watched them, asked about anything they carried, and searched their bags and boxes. But they ignored their clothing and the way several of them walked—stiff-legged, careful, slow.[90]

The tension was terrible. And when Lano asked Cox's press secretary about the box of framed family photos and wall hangings he was taking home, the man lost his temper. He pointed at the frame on top of the pile and said, "It's the Declaration of Independence, Angie. Just stamp it VOID and let me take it home."[91]

Archibald Cox did not return to the office. There was enough chaos without him adding to it. But he did send a message for the press. "Whether ours shall continue to be a government of laws and not of men is now for Congress, and ultimately the American people" to decide.

The American people knew what kind of government they wanted, and it wasn't the one they'd just seen. It was time to speak up.

CHAPTER 11

The People Speak
OCTOBER 1973–JULY 1974

T he people raised their voices before news coverage of the firing finished for the evening. Western Union, the telegram service, saw its computers suddenly overloaded and its telephone operators overwhelmed. Thousands of telegrams, ten times the usual number, poured into the White House and into Congress all through Saturday night and Sunday. They came from shocked and angry Americans.

At the same time, less than two hours after the announcement of the firings, protestors gathered in front of the White House. They held homemade signs reading "Honk for Impeachment." Passing drivers responded with blaring horns.

On Sunday morning, one of the protestors encouraging people to honk wore a prison costume and a Nixon mask as he stood in front of the White House. A couple walked back and forth, the man pushing a stroller with one hand and holding up an "Impeach Nixon" sign with the other. More people gathered in the park next to the White House and in front of the wrought iron fence that separated the White House grounds from the street.

But . . . isn't honking at the president and making signs and sending angry telegrams a bit disloyal? Unpatriotic?

No. It's not.

The United States Constitution begins, "We the People of the United States." When it comes to government, *We the People* may be the most important three words ever written. The US government gets its power from the people. As one delegate to the Constitutional Convention said in 1787, the president "is not the king. The people are the king."[92] Americans hire and pay the president, who then works for them. Franklin Roosevelt said, "I never forget that I live in a house owned by all the American people."[93]

Citizens of the United States have the right and the duty to be sure their president is living up to his or her oath. Nonviolently expressing concern and anger over presidential policies or actions that violate that oath is a patriotic act, a kind of activism or protest, and a way of defending the Constitution.

There are other ways to oversee the government. Informed voting, a citizen's right and responsibility, is the most obvious. Sending letters and e-mails to representatives in Congress and to the president can be effective too. Sometimes, though, a situation demands an immediate and loud response. That voice—the voice of *We the People*—can change the course of history.

The Sunday newspapers and news shows were filled with articles about what quickly became known as the "Saturday Night Massacre." The *Washington Post's* front page headlined four stories on the firings. So did the *New York Times's*. People in coffee shops and parks talked about what had happened. They didn't understand why Cox had been fired. They didn't accept that it was necessary. If Nixon was innocent of the accusations against him, why get rid of the man who could bring out the truth? And how did anyone, even a president, defy a court order?

Archibald Cox's staff members had gathered in small groups Saturday night and into Sunday morning, worried, nervous, and angry about what had happened and what they could do now. The image of sneaking evidence out in front of FBI agents at their offices played over and over in their minds. It didn't seem real. But that scene was only one piece of a bigger effort the staff had made to protect evidence. On Friday, the day before the firings, lawyers and other staffers had kept the copy machines running nonstop. Cox had encouraged them to stay on the job if he was fired, as he was sure he would be. To do that, they needed their files, memos, and legal papers. They couldn't let anyone destroy their work, so they made copies of what they could and took them home.

On Saturday, as the firings were announced, some staffers who sensed what was about to happen had rushed back to their offices. One lawyer filled his briefcase with critical documents and left before the FBI got there. He put the briefcase in the trunk of his car and then asked a friend for help. They hid the documents in a safe at the friend's office. The press secretary for the special prosecutor had been recording his notes each day as he drove home. On Saturday night, he collected all the tapes and got permission from a neighbor to hide them in her basement storage room in case the FBI showed up to search his house.[94]

On Sunday, members of the special prosecutor's staff arrived at the K Street office again. FBI agents stood inside the door and it took some convincing to get into the building. A television in the lobby showed a presidential advisor assuring a newsman that "the FBI is not present and has not sealed off those offices." An FBI agent watching the lobby television let the staff members pass.[95]

The president had said that he was abolishing or dissolving the special prosecutor's office. But Congress had authorized the office of the special prosecutor, and the staff members were government workers. The president hadn't appointed them and he couldn't simply fire them. Someone would have to complete a lot of paperwork and prove that the president could dismiss the staff. Someone would have to come tell the staffers they were fired or deliver documents firing them. That hadn't happened.

A reporter at the K Street building asked how the office could continue if it was abolished. Cox's press secretary answered, "The White House announced we were abolished. But . . . if they announce the sky is green and you look up and see the sky is blue . . ."[96] In other words, the staff would keep working until they had proof that the president had the authority to keep them from working.

That sounded brave, but the fact was that no one on the special prosecutor's staff knew if they would be able to continue for more than a day or two. They were almost ready to ask the grand jury to indict several people for serious crimes, and they had worked up strong court cases. They had evidence of criminal behavior by a number of high government officials. And all of it might be gone before the week was out. As one lawyer on Cox's team told a reporter, "One thinks that in a democracy maybe this would not happen."[97]

A few months earlier, during the summer of 1973, there had been some talk of impeachment—the bringing of formal charges against the president, similar to an indictment. But not many people liked the idea. It felt too extreme. Surely, there was a better way to deal with all the accusations. After all, Nixon was elected in a landslide and while public approval had dropped since then because of the scandal, most Americans did not think he should be impeached and removed from office.

Now, though, after the Saturday Night Massacre in late October, the public reconsidered what they thought about the president. Only a quarter of Americans still approved of the job he was doing. Editorials in the *New York Times* and several other newspapers around the country called on Nixon to resign. *Time*, the nation's top weekly news magazine, printed an editorial titled "The President Should Resign." It was the first opinion piece the magazine had ever printed in its fifty-year history.[98] The *Washington Post* called for impeachment.

Everywhere—in the news media, in protest chants

Demonstrators march to the US Capitol with posters demanding Nixon's impeachment, October 1973.

and on protest signs, in thousands of telegrams and calls—people heard and read the word *impeachment*. The very word rattled many Americans. Only one president had ever been impeached and that had been a hundred years earlier. It was frightening to think about impeaching Richard Nixon, and only one-third of Americans supported removing him from office even after the firings.[99] But one Republican member of the House of Representatives said, "Impeachment resolutions are going to be raining down like hailstones."[100]

How big of a deal is an impeachment anyway?

Article I, section 2, of the Constitution says, "The House of Representatives . . . shall have the sole power of impeachment." That's very clear. Section 3 goes on to say that "the Senate shall have the sole power to try all impeachments." In other words, the House of Representatives can vote to bring charges, described in *articles of impeachment*, against the president for violating the presidential oath or for illegal activity. If a majority of the House votes to impeach, there is a trial. The Senate acts as the jury in that trial. The chief justice of the Supreme Court acts as the judge. However, impeachment is different from the legal system. First, impeachment is a political action, not a legal action. The president does not have to break the law to face impeachment. The House can vote to impeach because they believe the president has violated his oath or abused his office or harmed the country with his behavior. And there are no set rules for how the Senate trial will proceed. While the chief justice acts to oversee the Senate trial, he or she does not have the same kind of authority to run the trial as the judge in a criminal trial does.

In an impeachment trial, the Senate can either find the president not guilty (acquitted) or guilty (convicted). If two-thirds of the Senate votes not guilty, the president goes on being president. But if two-thirds vote guilty, the president is removed from office. Then, if there is evidence that the former president has broken the law, he or she can be indicted, go to trial in a regular courtroom, and face prison time like anyone else.

As predicted, impeachment resolutions did rain down. On the Tuesday morning after the Saturday Night Massacre, twelve individual representatives in the House introduced resolutions seeking either impeachment proceedings or additional investigations or hearings.

At the same time, Judge Sirica said he was "plain, damned angry." He'd seen all the news on Saturday and Sunday and thought that sending the FBI to seal those offices looked like a *coup*. It felt like the kind of thing that happened in non-democratic, unstable countries where the military suddenly bursts into the capital and takes over. Sirica was taking no chances. He called in the members of the two Watergate grand juries and read out loud the oath each of those citizens had taken. "You will not be dismissed," he told them, "except by this court as provided by law."

Some people thought John Sirica was a little rough around the edges for a judge. But even his critics knew that no one had more respect for the rule of law. Once he finished with the grand juries, he called the lawyers from the special prosecutor's team into his chambers. "The law can take care of this situation," he told them. They should keep working.[101]

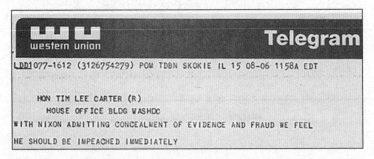

```
western union                          Telegram
LDD1077-1612 (3126754279) POM TDBN SKOKIE IL 15 08-06 1158A EDT

    HON TIM LEE CARTER (R)
       HOUSE OFFICE BLDG WASHDC
WITH NIXON ADMITTING CONCEALMENT OF EVIDENCE AND FRAUD WE FEEL
HE SHOULD BE IMPEACHED IMMEDIATELY
```

Hundreds of thousands of telegrams and calls flooded the Capitol and the White House in the days after Cox's firing.

• • •

Similarly, ordinary Americans just kept speaking. And writing. And honking. As the week went on, it was more than car horns penetrating the walls of the Oval Office and the First Family's residence upstairs. Drivers of eighteen-wheelers or big rigs blared their air horns. Police arrived to make sure the protestors stayed peaceful and to issue tickets for making too much noise. But even some of them honked the horns of their squad cars. Tour buses drove past the White House, and the tourists on board cheered drivers who leaned on the bus horns. Some passengers opened the bus windows so they could yell for impeachment.[102]

Richard Nixon couldn't take it. He started spending as much time as he could at Camp David, the presidential retreat in Maryland just a short helicopter ride away. The honking went on anyway. So did the calls and letters and telegrams—three hundred thousand telegrams in a week.

Nixon knew he had blundered. He'd handled the crisis in the Middle East with diplomatic skill and the serious threat of military force. At any other time, Americans might have been calling him a hero worthy of the Nobel Peace Prize. Instead, all anyone could talk about was Watergate and the Saturday Night Massacre.

Six days after the firings, Richard Nixon made another television appearance. Trying to defend himself and regain support, he announced that the crisis in the Middle

East was under control. He and his secretary of state had urged a cease-fire and avoided war with Russia. That was news everyone could cheer. Then he changed topics and explained that Archibald Cox had forced his own firing and he, the president, would have his acting attorney general appoint another special prosecutor. Even supporters didn't believe that Nixon had intended all along to have another special prosecutor. Clearly, the public firestorm of protest had been effective.

Days later, Nixon's lawyer surprised everyone when he told Judge Sirica that the White House had decided to turn over nine subpoenaed tapes. Before the country could think about it, though, the agreement fell apart. Two of the nine tapes the judge had demanded didn't exist. Were they missing? Never existed in the first place? Stolen? Destroyed? The answers were vague. But it seemed suspicious that the missing tapes were from days when the president had met in the Oval Office with John Dean. They were the tapes that could prove whether John Dean or the president was telling the truth.

Then the news got worse. A key recording of Nixon and his men, taped three days after the Watergate break-in, had an eighteen-minute gap. The president's lawyers offered theories on how such a thing could have happened, and Nixon's secretary demonstrated how she must have accidentally erased part of the tape when she reached to answer the phone. No one believed any of it. Later, a panel of technology experts determined that the tape showed five separate, intentional erasures. By then, two-thirds of Americans said they believed that all the important tapes had been doctored.[103]

The president's barricade was failing. He had misjudged how far toward total control he could go. The American people had made it clear that they wanted the truth and

President Nixon calls on reporters at a press conference, October 1973.

they wanted a president who followed the law. Nixon said in a press conference in November, "People have got to know whether or not their president is a crook. Well, I'm not a crook." But after all the lies that had come out over the last year and a half, was that just one more lie? The country had reached a point no one had ever wanted to reach.

CHAPTER 12

The House Investigates
NOVEMBER 1973–JULY 1974

I mpeachment. Americans across the country were talking about impeachment now. But even Americans in Congress didn't know much about the process. They needed to learn, and learn quickly.

Impeachment is the strongest check the legislative branch has on the executive branch—the final defense against a president's abuse of power. In late October 1973, the Judiciary Committee of the House of Representatives announced the beginning of an impeachment inquiry to answer one question: Should the House of Representatives, the only governmental body with the power to do so, impeach President Richard Nixon?

At the same time, a new special prosecutor took over where Cox had left off and continued the search for evidence of crimes while the grand jury issued more indictments. The Senate Watergate Committee continued its hearings as well, though without television coverage. But the Senate would still keep the public informed of their findings and then recommend changes in the law based on all that had happened.

The House Judiciary Committee's thirty-eight members had a different job. They had to decide if there was sufficient reason to call for an impeachment vote in the full House of Representatives and send the president of the United States to trial in the Senate. It was a frightening responsibility.

Peter Rodino had represented Newark, New Jersey, in the House for twenty-six years, but hardly anyone outside his home district knew his name. He didn't give big speeches or introduce historic pieces of legislation. He didn't plan to run for president. At sixty-four, he was content with his role in Congress. He often worked behind the scenes, writing sections of voting rights laws and quietly but firmly pushing his colleagues to vote in favor of civil rights legislation and immigration reform. He didn't need public credit for that kind of work. He just wanted important laws passed.

In November 1973, Rodino had chaired the House Judiciary Committee for less than a year. He was keenly aware that no one had voted for him to be chair—he just happened to be on the committee longer than any other Democrat. Now he was undertaking a task he'd never bargained for.

The south wing of the US Capitol, where the House of Representatives meets

Rodino grew up in the Little Italy section of Newark—a neighborhood filled with Italian immigrants like his father, who worked as a carpenter. A lot of the older people there had a hard time learning English. Many weren't educated, and no one had much money. But Peter Rodino, despite losing his mother at four and struggling financially, was determined to get an education and make a good life. He worked his way through a local college, studied law at night, and married his high school sweetheart. During World War II, he saw combat in North Africa and Italy where his fluent Italian was a great asset to the US Army. He came home to Newark a hero with the promotions and medals to prove it. Rodino won his first election to Congress in 1948 and won a dozen more elections after. He kept winning even as his district changed and he represented more Puerto Ricans and African Americans than Italian Americans. They knew him as a good man.

As House Judiciary Committee chair, Rodino thought the key to the inquiry's success was hiring an excellent staff the way the Senate committee and the special prosecutor had done. He turned to John Doar, a tall, skinny lawyer from Wisconsin whose blue eyes seemed always intense. Doar had spent the 1960s risking his life as a civil rights attorney in the Department of Justice. He put himself in one dangerous situation after another, determined to end segregation in the American South. Now he would lead a team of over a hundred men and women to give the House Judiciary Committee an impartial, unbiased, fair look at the president's conduct in office. That's what Peter Rodino wanted. Doar insisted that he would not hire anyone for his team who had "expressed an opinion or judgment on Richard Nixon one way or the other." Their job was "to get the facts." Later, he said, "My job was to make the Constitution work. Whether to a trial or to a vindication [finding of innocence] didn't matter."[104]

Rodino started preparations for the committee's work right away. He studied the gigantic records of the Senate hearings and the special prosecutor's investigation. He read and reread a history of the nation's only presidential impeachment at the time—Andrew Johnson's in 1868. In that case, 105 years earlier, the House of Representatives voted to impeach Andrew Johnson. But the Senate, by one vote, found Johnson not guilty and he remained president until the end of his term. Rodino wanted to understand every detail.

The problem for Rodino and the other members of the House Judiciary Committee was that no one alive in 1973 had any experience with presidential impeachment. The Senate committee's task was clear: inform the public and propose changes in the law. The special prosecutors' task was also clear: prosecute people who had broken the law. But Rodino's task, impeachment, was less clear.

Rodino read the US Constitution, Article II, section 4.

The President, Vice President and all civil Officers of the United States, shall be removed from
Office on Impeachment for, and Conviction
of, Treason, Bribery, or other high Crimes and
Misdemeanors.

Treason is defined very specifically in the Constitution.
Bribery is defined in law books. But high crimes and misdemeanors? No one was too sure what those were exactly.

Rodino and other committee members found copies of
Edmund Burke's writings from eighteenth-century England.
They looked for volumes of the Federalist Papers by James
Madison, Alexander Hamilton, and John Jay—essays that
explained the framers' thinking on the Constitution. Rodino
couldn't stop. He needed to know more. He worked most
days from six thirty in the morning until well past midnight.
In the meantime, John Doar hired bright young lawyers and
experienced investigators. They debated the meaning of the
Constitution and the law. They pieced together information
from thousands of pages of documents. As they worked,
Richard Nixon's situation continued to worsen.

In late 1973, oil shortages made gasoline and heating fuel
expensive and hard to get. People talked about the "energy
crisis" and blamed the president. In early December,

Republican representative Gerald Ford of Michigan, who had been in Congress for twenty-five years, was sworn in as the new vice president. That was a good thing since Ford was a strong Nixon defender and Nixon needed a new vice president after Agnew's resignation. But having a vice president, someone to take over should the president leave office, also made it easier for everyone to think about impeachment.

And then came a huge insult, at least in Nixon's mind. Judge John Sirica—the judge who demanded the tapes, ruled against the president, and told Nixon's aides to cooperate with the Senate—appeared on the cover of *Time* magazine as Man of the Year. Could anything else happen before 1973 was over? Yes, it could.

Three of the tapes Nixon's lawyer had turned over to the court went to the grand jury. One of them was the recording of the conversation John Dean said he had with the president the previous March. Now the new special prosecutor—Leon Jaworski—and the lawyers on his staff heard the tape.

"The crimes came spilling out," one lawyer said later, "one on top of another."[105] Bribery, hush money, perjury. The president and his men discussed it all. Nixon and his chief of staff had claimed over and over that at that meeting the president said "it would be wrong" to pay anyone to keep quiet. But that's not what was there on the tape. The president had said no such thing. Instead, the lawyers listened as Richard Nixon coached his men on what to say under oath.

Jaworski's face reddened. "Can you imagine that?" he said. "The president of the United States sitting in his office telling his staff how to commit perjury."[106] It seemed John Dean had a remarkable memory and, more important, had been telling the truth. Jaworski quietly told the president's new chief of staff, "You should get the finest criminal lawyer you can find . . . and let him study the tapes."

Investigations continued all over Washington through the end of the year and into 1974. In the House, in the special prosecutor's office, and in the news media. Bob Woodward and Carl Bernstein wrote four or five front-page articles nearly every week—articles uncovering new information about the missing tapes, the erased tapes, the Cox firing, wiretaps, and more. Other media outlets kept a close eye on the Nixon White House too. The only good news for the president was that the public was getting tired of Watergate all over again. It felt like it had no end, and paying close attention seemed a bit like standing in the ocean letting wave after wave hit but never turning away. It was easier to ignore it all, especially through the holiday season.

The men and women conducting the investigation for John Doar and the members of the House Judiciary Committee, Peter Rodino included, didn't have that choice, no matter how worn out they felt. In February, after nearly three months of work, worry, and little sleep, Rodino fell ill. He spent almost a week in the hospital, suffering exhaustion, difficulty breathing, and chest pain. He hadn't asked for this impeachment responsibility, but he'd done his best leading the House Judiciary Committee. Maybe his best wasn't enough. He'd never been a star in Congress. Maybe . . .

One of Rodino's doctors stepped away from his physician role and spoke simply as an American. "We need you," he told the congressman.[107] Rodino had asked himself, "Why me?" more than once since late October. The doctor's answer would have to do. The country didn't need a star leading the impeachment inquiry. It needed Peter Rodino, who was known for being patient, fair, and thoughtful. He had to recover and get back to work.

Pressure on Nixon continued into the spring. In March, the grand jury indicted seven of the president's former top aides, including men who had testified so arrogantly before the Senate. The fifty-page document brought charges against the men for conspiracy, perjury, obstructing justice, and more. Those indictments were public information.

The next day, the *Washington Post* reported that since the Watergate break-in in June 1972, twenty-eight White House and CRP men, including the seven just indicted, faced formal charges related to Watergate and the other investigations. At that rate, who was left to do the actual business of government?

Next, a committee reviewing the president's tax returns revealed that Nixon had lied about his income and had charged the government, meaning ordinary taxpayers, more than $90,000 for personal expenses including a $5,000 party for his daughter.

In April, Peter Rodino's committee subpoenaed forty tapes of presidential conversations. Special Prosecutor Leon Jaworski asked for even more tapes a few days later. Nixon again refused to turn them over, but this time offered to give the committee and the public the transcripts—written versions—of those conversations. At the end of the month, he went on television to tell everyone what he was doing and to admit that the transcripts, sitting behind him in fancy binders, would be embarrassing to him. But they would prove that he had not known about the cover-up until John Dean told him in March 1973.

President Nixon gives a televised address with binders of tape transcripts beside him, April 29, 1974.

Nixon believed that Americans would not have the time, patience, or interest to read the 250,000 words he was about to release. A thousand pages of tedious dialogue they wouldn't care about. He was probably right that few people had the patience for the whole thing. But he was wrong that they didn't care. The upcoming House debate and recent stories in the news had recaptured people's attention. When they read bits and pieces of the transcripts, the words focused their anger and upset toward the president all over again.

Within days of the transcripts' release, people across the country were talking about the president's foul language and coarse speech. Newspapers and magazines quoted chunks of the transcripts, and the *Washington Post* and *New York Times* quickly printed them as books that sold as fast as they could be produced. Nixon was always such a gentleman in public, people said. But in private . . .

On page after page of Nixon's conversations, readers saw "[expletive deleted]" replacing easy-to-guess curse words. The expression became a joke on late-night shows and in offices and among friends.

Most of what Americans saw, though, wasn't a joke. It was hundreds of different bits of disturbing, unsettling information. Their president, elected in a landslide, sounded angry and bitter. He constantly used racial and ethnic slurs or insults. He insulted Jews, immigrants, African Americans—pretty much anyone who wasn't just like him. And he ranted and raged against the press, the Democrats, and everyone else involved in investigating Watergate. If Nixon spent this much time talking about Watergate and who was out to get him, people thought, he couldn't be payng close attention to presidential work.

One conservative publisher called the transcripts "as damning a document as it is possible to imagine . . . ruthless, deplorable, and ethically indefensible. . . ."

A Republican senator called them "disgusting, shabby, and immoral."[108]

Worst of all, millions of Americans realized that the man they entrusted with the most powerful job in the world wasn't the man they thought he was. The flag pin on his lapel and the sincere speeches he made meant nothing. They recognized that never once in all those 250,000 words did Richard Nixon question the morality, the right or wrong, of what he and his men were doing. Never.

Peter Rodino and his legal staff didn't have time to joke about foul language or feel disgusted. They didn't have time to find the right adjectives to describe the transcripts either. There was only one adjective that mattered—dishonest. They carefully compared the written transcripts to the nine actual tapes they'd received from the grand jury and found huge differences.

Where the transcript said "I didn't know about it," the actual tape recording of the conversation said, "I did know about it." Where the transcript said "In order to get off the cover-up line," the president really said, "In order to get on with the cover-up."[109] The doctoring went on and on as the American people had suspected. It was a clear case of illegal tampering with evidence. Another crime. How could anyone even feel shocked anymore? Crimes in the Oval Office, the president's crimes, now seemed routine.

A staffer for Sam Dash, a young woman whose father

objected when she took the job investigating the president, was furious. Her father was a modest man, a hardworking man who believed in the United States government. He'd voted for Richard Nixon twice and supported him through the last two years. But now, when he read those transcripts, he realized that terrible things were going on at the White House. He called his daughter and told her he was sorry. It wasn't easy for a proud man to say that and she could hear the pain in his voice.[110] How dare the president hurt a good man this way, she thought. How dare he hurt the country this way?

Nixon had now defied multiple subpoenas—from the Senate committee, from the House committee, and from two special prosecutors. Patience had run out. It was time to involve the nation's highest court.

CHAPTER 13

The Supreme Court Rules

JULY 1974

A t a glance, Monday, July 8, 1974, looked like an ordinary summer morning in Washington, DC. Tourists gathered near the base of the Capitol to see the inside of the enormous dome. Others leaned on the cool stone of the Washington Monument or climbed the steps of the Lincoln Memorial to measure themselves against the statue of the great man.

People also lined up in front of the marble-columned building that houses the National Archives. They stood outside in the heat and humidity, chatting and planning what to do next. But conversations faded to near silence when they walked through the massive doors to the darkened chamber and saw the shatterproof, moisture-proof, bulletproof glass and steel cases that protect and preserve America's founding documents. This was a hallowed place. A place to show respect.

No visitor *needed* to see original copies of the Declaration of Independence, the US Constitution, and the Bill of Rights, of course. They could find the words in school-books or pocket-size pamphlets (and online today). They knew the text—"all men are created equal"; "in order to form a more perfect union"; "freedom of speech." But looking at the faded, mostly illegible, handwritten documents was special. There it was, the world's oldest written plan for government still in use anywhere. *We the People*—the constitutional system that had worked for nearly two hundred years, even surviving the terrible Civil War. But on this day, many Americans weren't so sure about the future and whether their government would go on as they'd always thought it would. The nation's capital may have looked like it did on any ordinary summer morning, but there was unusual tension in the air. A sense of anticipation. Worry.

Just down the block from the National Archives and across the street from the Capitol, hundreds of men and women stood on the sidewalk in front of the Supreme Court Building. A few of them had staked out their spots two days earlier to be at the head of the line. Heat already rippled through the morning haze, and the humid air felt thick. But they waited patiently.

By nine o'clock an ice cream truck was there selling frozen treats.[111] Popsicles went fast despite the early hour, offering a welcome bit of coolness in the hot sun. The people buying them knew they might be in line for a very long time. They weren't there to see the usual tourist sights this Monday morning. Instead, each of them hoped to witness history being made as the justices of the Supreme Court heard arguments in the case of *United States v. Richard M. Nixon, President of the United States.*

Heard arguments? What exactly does the Supreme Court do?

The Constitution spells out the duties and powers of the legislative and executive branches of government. It also says that judicial power in the United States will be in the courts. But the Constitution does not specifically define the role of the Supreme Court.

Generally, the Supreme Court acts as the nation's highest court of appeals. It does not conduct trials or determine anyone's guilt or innocence. Instead, the Supreme Court decides if a law or government action is constitutional, meaning that it follows the Constitution. If it is *un*constitutional, violating the Constitution, the Supreme Court *strikes* the law. The law no longer exists. The Supreme Court, like appeals courts, also *interprets* the Constitution and the law, saying what the words of the Constitution or law mean.

The Supreme Court hears only a hundred or so of the thousands of cases it is asked to hear each year. The court decides which those will be. Lawyers from each side of a case give the court their written arguments or briefs before the day of the hearing. The nine justices study the briefs and then listen to both sides' oral arguments and ask questions at the hearing. But they don't make any decision at the hearing itself. Most decisions or opinions are announced months later. However, in *United States v. Richard M. Nixon*, the court had agreed to hear the case in early July (they usually hear cases from October to June) and make a decision as quickly as possible.

United States v. Richard M. Nixon. The name of the case sounded ominous, as if pieces of government were battling each other. They were. And they had been for months. In late May, the Supreme Court had agreed to get involved at the request of Special Prosecutor Leon Jaworski. Now, on July 8, the justices would listen to arguments related to one question: Did the president have to turn over the subpoenaed tapes or not?

It sounded like a simple question, but the answer

Hundreds wait outside the Supreme Court Building for a chance to witness history, July 8, 1974

depended on other questions, complicated questions. The people outside on the sidewalk, as well as politicians, professors, journalists, and millions of ordinary Americans, hoped this case would answer those complicated questions. Are the three branches of government really equal? Or does the president have more authority than Congress or the Supreme Court? Or is the separation of power something else altogether? Does the president have to follow the laws Congress passes the same way other people do? Or are there exceptions for the president? If there are, how far do they go? Is there such a thing as executive privilege? Who determines what documents, if any, a president can keep private? The Supreme Court faced a difficult task.

Everyone standing in line in front of the Supreme Court Building knew that the odds of getting into the chamber where the justices meet weren't good. Most seats would be taken up by presidential and legal aides, invited guests, members of Congress, and reporters. Those members of the public who *were* ushered in could stand in the back of the room for only minutes before the next group took their place. Many of the people waiting in the heat would be disappointed. The hearing would be over before they had a chance to go inside at all.

The odds didn't matter. The men and women who'd come for the hearing believed that this case was so important they had to try to see the justices in person and hear some small part of the arguments made before the court. At the least, they could be near the event. When Special Prosecutor Leon Jaworski and some of his staff approached the steps of the Supreme Court Building, the crowd of people outside broke into applause and one man shouted, "Go USA!"[112] Was he cheering for the special prosecutor's arguments against Nixon's position? Or for the system of government that he believed would settle the issue peacefully? Or something else? Jaworski kept walking toward the court's massive doors.

Leon Jaworski had been the Watergate special prosecutor since early November 1973. He'd come to Washington from Texas to accept the job two weeks after Nixon had Cox fired. The newest attorney general promised Jaworski complete independence if he took the position. But his wife said, "It's a terrible job. I just feel sorry for him."[113]

Nixon had had no choice. If he didn't tell his attorney general to appoint a new special prosecutor with a good reputation as an attorney, Congress would appoint someone. At least this way, the White House had some say in who it would be. Nixon's men had gone through lists of possibilities. It wasn't easy—not many people would accept the job at this point. But Jaworski looked good to them. He'd acknowledged that he voted for Richard Nixon twice, but he was a Democrat, which would please the Democratic majority in Congress. He was a conservative, however, when it came to defense and security issues, and Nixon's aides hoped they could lean on Jaworski's patriotism to convince him to stay away from areas that the president said were national security concerns. They also knew that Nixon would like the fact that Jaworski wasn't an East Coast, elite, Ivy League guy. He was a Texan.

The staff at the special prosecutor's office had been hesitant to accept Jaworski. Nearly everyone in the office felt tremendous respect and admiration for Archibald Cox. They were fond of him and outraged at the way the White House had treated him. They worried that Leon Jaworski wouldn't measure up.

Jaworski had finished law school at the top of his class when he was nineteen years old. He was the youngest person ever licensed to practice law in Texas. Thirty years later, he had one of the two or three most successful law firms in the country. He'd also been president of the American Bar Association, a national organization most lawyers belong to. The staff knew he was smart and a good lawyer—that wasn't the problem. He had an excellent reputation. Their concern was that Jaworski had spent years with very high-powered people and worked for President Lyndon Johnson, whom he considered a friend. They were afraid that his enormous respect for the presidency would prevent him from digging for the evidence no matter what it meant for Richard Nixon.[114]

It was a good sign, then, when Jaworski and others on the team heard the three tapes Nixon turned over to Judge Sirica just after Jaworski started his new job. He'd been as shocked as anyone else as he heard the president telling

Special prosecutor Leon Jaworski asked the Supreme Court to decide if the president could refuse to turn over subpoenaed material.

his men to lie under oath. And after he studied the evidence the team had collected and saved, he let them know he was as determined as Cox had been to find the truth.

Jaworski had strong feelings about democracy and how fragile democratic governments are. He had seen firsthand how the people of a nation can lose their liberty and rights. It had happened in Nazi Germany in the 1930s and had led to World War II. After the war ended in 1945, Leon Jaworski went to Germany with other lawyers to prosecute war crimes—actions that violate rules for warfare that most nations have agreed to. He saw what had happened in Germany, where Adolf Hitler led his country into the *Holocaust*—the government-led persecution and murder of six million Jews, as well as millions of other people Hitler labeled "inferior." How could anything so horrific happen? How could the people of a nation *let* it happen?

Jaworski had concluded that it came about little by little, one step at a time. Jews and others lost one small freedom and then another and another until the Nazi government turned to mass murder. The people of Germany weren't bad any more than any other nation's people are, Jaworski believed. But bit by bit they'd stopped paying attention to what their government was doing because it was easier not to know. It was easier to accept the propaganda and the conspiracy stories and the blame games about Jews than to fight back and risk losing a job or home or worse. It was safer to look the other way and not question the government's morality. Those who did fight back or ask questions went to prison or disappeared. By the time it became impossible to pretend the horror didn't exist, it was too late to stop it. Hitler's henchmen were everywhere, and the only way to survive was to stay quiet while millions of innocent people were murdered.

Jaworski thought that the people in Germany probably would have stood up to something huge and sudden like a military takeover or revolution that threatened everyone. But they hadn't stood up to a series of movements in a very wrong direction that, at first, didn't threaten them directly or personally. Jaworski saw the beginnings of that same attitude in some of the Watergate testimony. More than one White House aide or staffer for the Committee to Reelect the President said that in the White House and in CRP, seeing the president succeed was more important than any person's individual rights.[115] They knew they were breaking the law when it came to secret funds and bugging offices and the rest, but they convinced themselves it was okay. Besides, they wanted to keep their White House jobs and the prestige that went with them.

Leon Jaworski knew the terrible danger in that kind of thinking. Americans could lose their most basic freedoms— freedom of speech and the press and assembly, the right to vote in a free and fair election, the right to privacy. They could lose their democracy, their republic, one step at a time. There was no telling where it would stop.

Over a period of weeks and months, Jaworski proved himself to the special prosecutor team. They continued to uncover volumes of evidence and debated every aspect of the case against the president and his men. In the process, they requested more of the president's tapes but got no cooperation from the White House even after Judge Sirica issued a subpoena in late May. That was when Jaworski asked the Supreme Court to step in.

Now, on July 8, with the chamber full of spectators and hundreds of people waiting outside, Jaworski and Philip Lacovara, one of the young lawyers on the special prosecutor team, were ready to argue their case. They and the president's attorney had given the justices written versions of their arguments ahead of time. The justices had read them and now asked questions as each side presented its case.

Impeachments are political events, Lacovara said, speaking for the special prosecutor. But the demand for the tapes was not political. It had nothing to do with impeachment and had started long before the Congressional impeachment investigation going on across the street at the Capitol. The special prosecutor needed the tapes to conduct a *criminal* investigation, and the court needed to determine whose interpretation of executive privilege was correct. The president said only *he* could decide what information was privileged. But interpreting the law—interpreting the Constitution—is the court's job.

It has been the court's job as far back as 1803, when Chief Justice John Marshall said it is "emphatically the . . . duty" of the court "to say what the law is."[116]

Then the arguments were over and there was nothing to do but wait for the court's decision.

Lacovara left Washington for a well-earned but brief vacation with his family. Leon Jaworski stayed in town, missing his family and hoping his team had argued well enough. He thought they had.

Normally, months pass between the time the Supreme Court hears arguments in a case and the time the justices vote and issue the court's decision. One justice writes an explanation of that decision or majority opinion. If the vote is not unanimous, justices who voted in the minority against the decision sometimes explain their disagreement or *dissent* in writing. But the justices struggled with their usual process when it came to *United States v. Richard M. Nixon*.

First, the court could not wait months to issue its opinion. The country needed a resolution to the constitutional crisis it faced. And second, all the justices agreed that any dissent could be a disaster.

Months earlier, the president had said he would obey a "definitive" order from the court. No one knew exactly

what he meant. But now, in a rare move, the chief justice wrote the opinion and then other justices revised and
rewrote it until all were satisfied. On July 23, less than two
weeks after hearing the case, the Supreme Court announced
that it would make its opinion public the next day.

Leon Jaworski, Philip Lacovara, and other members of
the staff took seats in the chamber on July 24. So did lawyers from the president's team, as well as congressmen and
reporters. Despite the short notice, a line of people waited
outside on the court's steps and spilled onto the sidewalk
and around the corner as they had two weeks earlier. Just
after eleven o'clock, the justices entered the chamber and
Chief Justice Warren Burger, whom Nixon had appointed
as chief justice, prepared to read the decision.

The court had ruled unanimously that every president
has a constitutional right to protect the confidentiality of
his conversations. But that right "does not mean that all
material . . . is immune [protected] in all circumstances."
Criminal prosecutions have to be able to get to the facts.
And in this case, the criminal justice system was more
important than Nixon's claims to privacy in all communications. The president was not above the law.[117]

A unanimous Supreme Court had ordered Richard
Nixon to give up the tapes.

. . .

Special Prosecutor Leon Jaworski left the Supreme Court Building only minutes later, but news of the decision was already out. As he crossed the wide plaza in the oven-hot air, he found the marble stairs and the sidewalks below filled with reporters and cheering Americans. An embarrassed grin spread across his broad face. He'd won, and he admitted that he felt "right good" about it, but this wasn't something to celebrate.[118] For one thing, no one yet knew whether the president would obey the court's order. Or whether he'd continue to fight against the system.

Nixon had been away from Washington during the last part of June and most of July. He claimed that the trips he'd made to the Middle East and the Soviet Union had promoted world peace. But a lot of people suspected he'd just wanted to escape the tension in the nation's capital. When the Supreme Court issued its opinion, Nixon was at his home in San Clemente, California, where he'd been for over a week with his chief of staff, Alexander Haig, and other aides. On the morning of July 24, Nixon was in the office he'd built a short distance away from his villa. He was sitting alone, something he'd been doing more and more in recent months.

Haig dreaded telling the president that the Supreme Court had ruled against him in a unanimous decision. He had no choice, but he worried about Nixon's reaction.

Richard Nixon's home in San Clemente, California

Shortly before noon eastern time, nine o'clock a.m. in California, Haig went to the president's office.

Back in Washington, the special prosecutor's staff and members of the House Judiciary Committee waited and wondered. An hour passed, then two, then three. They heard nothing from the president. Maybe he needed time to get used to the idea of handing over the tapes. Maybe he was trying to work out a new strategy to avoid handing them over. Or maybe, just maybe, Richard

Nixon was preparing to refuse the Supreme Court's order.

Finally, at seven o'clock in the evening, the message came. Nixon's lawyer went on television to read a statement from the president. It was a paragraph long, but the important words were brief. "I respect and accept the court's decision." The entire city of Washington heaved a sigh of relief. But there was a catch. Nixon's lawyer finished the statement and then added, ". . . the time-consuming process" of preparing the tapes "will begin forthwith."[119]

Time-consuming? How long could it take to put a bunch of recording tapes in a box and carry them to K Street? Leon Jaworski had expected that Richard Nixon would try to drag this out as long as he could. But not if Jaworski could help it. The special prosecutor had gone from the Supreme Court Building to lunch and then back to his office early in the afternoon. By the time Nixon's lawyer read the statement and mentioned the time-consuming process, Jaworski and his staff had already written their arguments for a quick turnover of the tapes. They would present their brief to Judge Sirica— still overseeing the entire Watergate case in the district court as he had been for two years now—first thing in the morning. With the Supreme Court ruling on his side, Leon Jaworski was not going to accept any more delays.

CHAPTER 14

Debating Impeachment
JULY–AUGUST 1974

Monday, July 24, 1974, was a busy day in more than one way. The Supreme Court had handed down its decision a little before noon. Richard Nixon finally responded to the ruling through his lawyer just after seven p.m. And the House Judiciary Committee had scheduled its debate on impeachment for seven thirty. Committee Chairman Peter Rodino waited to find out what Nixon would do while television crews set up cameras in the committee's meeting room. Thirty minutes after hearing the president's response, it was time to begin. Rodino and the other members of the committee had been moving toward this moment all summer.

For weeks, Republicans as well as Democrats had studied the thirty-six binders filled with "statements of information" from Chief Counsel John Doar and his staff. After working all day, members often met in smaller groups to discuss the issues over dinner. Many representatives then took stacks of papers home with them. They went through the framers' writings. They requested books on narrow constitutional subjects no one had mentioned in over a century. They all believed they had to get this right. But they differed on what that meant.

The committee would debate and then vote on articles of impeachment, similar to charges in an indictment for crimes such as burglary. Any articles that the committee passed would go to the entire House of Representatives. If they passed there, the president would face trial in the Senate. Every member of the committee felt the weight of that responsibility.

House Judiciary Committee Chairman Peter Rodino (center-left) and Chief Counsel John Doar (center-right) answer reporters' questions, 1974.

. . .

A week earlier, staff counsel John Doar had presented a summary of the case that he and his staff had written. He didn't give the thirty-eight members of the House Judiciary Committee new information—they'd seen all the facts already—but his report explained the case clearly. Doar had included several possible articles of impeachment. The committee could revise or change them, but Doar's work gave them a starting point.

Of the seventeen Republicans on the House Judiciary Committee, six thought they might vote in favor of impeachment. Might. They'd been getting together quietly to discuss their thoughts and feelings, and the evidence. Even as juries convicted one after another of Nixon's men, several members still hoped the president was not guilty. Despite the stacks of documents, some insisted that the "evidence didn't add up," according to Republican Hamilton Fish. He added, "The question is 'Didn't add up to what?'"[120]

What action is impeachable? How bad does it have to be?

That's where the Constitution isn't clear. And it's important to understand that in 1787 the words "high crimes and misdemeanors" did not mean what they usually do in our speech today. A high crime wasn't a serious illegal act like murder or stealing millions of dollars. It was a crime against the nation. And a misdemeanor didn't mean a small crime like spray-painting a mailbox or stealing a bag of chips. It meant something that might not break a specific law but that was harmful to the country.[121] The framers wanted to put checks on presidents who broke the law and also on presidents who misused or abused their power and harmed the country whether that president broke a specific law or not. It's possible for a president to violate the presidential oath without violating the law. And violating that oath is reason enough for removal from office.

Doar talked to the committee about "enormous crimes" and "the terrible deed of subverting [weakening] the Constitution."[122] He said that the committee had to answer one question: Would the country and the Constitution be saved? It was up to the committee to take the facts he and his team had gathered and decide what to do next.

A reporter noticed that Doar was looking paler and older every week.[123] The work on this case had been very hard on John Doar, as it had been on so many people. It didn't help when the president's press secretary accused Doar, a Republican, of acting in a "partisan [political], duplicitous [dishonest], false way."[124]

Republicans on the committee didn't think John Doar was dishonest or false at all. But they and some Southern Democrats wanted more proof of Nixon's guilt. Something specific and undeniable—what the president's lawyer called "a smoking gun." They all knew the charges against the president would include obstruction of justice. That charge would say Nixon had kept evidence from the committee and the special prosecutor and had tried to influence the burglars to stay quiet. They also knew there would be a charge of abuse of power. That would include using government agencies to slow the investigation and go after enemies. And the committee would address the issue of defying subpoenas as well.

But most Republicans and several Democrats on the committee said that their votes would depend on the exact wording of each charge and the specific evidence. They weren't satisfied with the articles of impeachment Doar had suggested.

Committee members met all through the weekend of July 22 and 23. They expressed their concerns with each of the proposed articles of impeachment. They offered suggestions, additions, deletions. The undecided Republicans focused on the details they could vote for. Democrats offered other ideas. And a group of both Republicans and Democrats spent the last hours before the start of the committee's impeachment debate rewriting the document. But there was still more to do before they'd be ready to vote.[125]

At 7:44 on the evening of July 24, Peter Rodino banged the gavel to open the House Judiciary Committee's debate. He knew the articles of impeachment they would vote on weren't quite finalized yet. But tonight was reserved for the members' televised opening statements. They could begin while the staff kept working on the final document.

Rodino had overcome the early doubts about his ability to head the impeachment inquiry. Both Democrats and Republicans praised him for his leadership. They

The Senate Watergate Committee opens its hearings as members of Congress, aides, spectators, reporters, and television crews crowd the Senate Caucus Room, May 1973.

agreed that he'd created an atmosphere where members respected sincere differences of opinion. He'd brought dignity to the process.

Peter Rodino hadn't wanted the responsibility of an impeachment inquiry. But for eight months, he had managed to keep the committee focused on the Constitution. He'd made sure they thought about the way their actions would influence history and the future of the United States government. Now he let the country know that this was a solemn moment, no matter how they felt about Richard Nixon.

> Throughout all of the painstaking proceedings of this committee, I as the chairman have been guided by a simple principle, the principle that the law must deal fairly with every man. For me, this is the oldest principle of democracy ... Our judgment is not concerned with an individual but with a system of constitutional government ... Let us leave the Constitution as unimpaired for our children as our predecessors left it to us.[126]

Each of the thirty-eight members of the committee had fifteen minutes to speak before the vote. Many wanted to explain themselves. To tell the people who'd voted for them how they arrived at their decisions. But thirty-eight times fifteen is 570 minutes, or nine and a half hours. How many people around the country would pay attention to even a tenth of the debate? Rodino couldn't control that. But he wanted to be certain that Americans had the opportunity to hear their representatives speak about the Constitution and the law.

One Republican from New York said that he was not convinced that the president was personally involved. Another, from New Jersey, demanded, "Is there direct evidence that he had anything to do with it? Of course there is not."

Then a Democrat and former FBI agent acknowledged that he had supported Nixon years earlier. Now, though, he believed that the president had "consciously and intentionally engaged in serious misdeeds" and should be impeached.

Anyone keeping track at home could see that the debate was moving along party lines. Democrats thought the evidence against Nixon was strong. Republicans thought it was weak.

Rodino called on Republican Thomas Railsback of Illinois. Railsback talked about being Richard Nixon's friend. He said the president had campaigned for him and done "many wonderful things." But abuse of power isn't about friendship, he said. It isn't about being liberal or conservative. Railsback listed facts about Nixon's actions that troubled him, facts that he believed should trouble anyone. The congressman didn't say he was going to vote to impeach, but few people doubted his intention.

The speeches continued the next day. Members of the House committee shared their beliefs and philosophies through eight hours of careful, thoughtful speeches on the meaning of the Constitution.

Conservative Southern Democrat Walter Flowers admitted that the decision-making in the case was difficult. He said he'd been waking up at night wondering if the idea of impeaching the president of the United States was all a bad dream. The stress had caused his ulcer (an open sore in the stomach) to flare up. He said that he and most Americans wanted to support the president. But what would happen if they didn't impeach? What would it mean for the future of the country? He listed the values the Constitution upholds—liberty, justice . . . Then he said, "Our problem is not now to find better values, our problem is to be faithful to those we profess—and to make them live in modern times."

Republican Caldwell Butler of Virginia also spoke about the loyalty he owed Nixon. He wouldn't be in Congress if it weren't for Nixon, he said. But in the end, the "misuse of power is the very essence of tyranny." He'd heard and seen enough evidence and could not "stand still."[127] He explained,

> If we fail to impeach, we will have condoned and left unpunished a course of conduct totally inconsistent with the reasonable expectations of the American people . . . and we will have said to the American people, "These deeds are inconsequential and unimportant."[128]

The speeches went on all day. Millions of Americans tuned in for at least some part of the broadcast. People watching got the feeling they'd stepped back into the Constitutional Convention of 1787. Most had never heard of a lot of these members of Congress, and they were impressed with their language and passion.

By evening, the committee members were exhausted. But people at home kept watching. There was one person they especially wanted to hear.

Democrat Barbara Jordan was one of just sixteen women in the 435-member House of Representatives (today, over one hundred women serve in the House). She was a former Texas state judge with a reputation for being very smart and very well-spoken. Now she began to talk, her deep voice clear and strong.

House Judiciary Committee member Barbara Jordan
spoke passionately about her oath to protect and defend
the Constitution.

Jordan said that as a black woman, she was not
included in the original meaning of *We the People*. But
amendments, court decisions, and new interpretations
had brought her to Congress. Her faith in the Constitution, she said, "is whole, it is complete, it is total. And I
am not going to sit here and be an idle spectator to the
diminution [shrinking], the subversion, the destruction
of the Constitution." Barbara Jordan had meant it when
she swore to "support and defend the Constitution of
the United States." Struck by the power of her words,

some people watching at home cheered and applauded right there in front of their televisions.[129]

All the while, John Doar and his staff worked on the articles of impeachment. Several members of the committee joined them once the debate paused for the evening. Peter Rodino wanted a *bipartisan* (both Democrats and Republicans) vote. If all Democrats voted for the articles and all Republicans voted against, the articles would pass. But if that happened, the whole process would look like simple, ugly politics. Rodino wanted to show the American people that the House Judiciary Committee took its constitutional responsibilities more seriously than that. He hoped the full House of Representatives would do the same when the time came.

Finally, after working through three sleepless nights, the committee pushed the articles of impeachment into the best wording possible. The thirty-eight members of the committee met to vote on Friday, July 26.

Article I, Obstruction of Justice.

In his conduct of the office of President of the United States, Richard M. Nixon, in violation of his constitutional oath faithfully to execute the office of President of the United States, and, to the best of his ability, preserve, protect, and defend the Constitution of the United States, and in violation of his constitutional duty to take care that the laws be faithfully executed, has prevented, obstructed and impeded the administration of justice, in that:

On June 17, 1972, and prior thereto, agents of the Committee for the Reelection of the President:

Committed unlawful entry of the headquarters of the Democratic National Committee in Washington, District of Columbia, for the purpose of securing political intelligence. Subsequent thereto, Richard M. Nixon, using the powers of his high office, engaged personally and through his subordinates and agents in a course of conduct or plan designed to delay, impede, and obstruct the investigation of such unlawful entry; to cover up, conceal, and protect those responsible; and to conceal the existence and scope of other unlawful covert activities. . . . Wherefore Richard M. Nixon, by such conduct, warrants impeachment and trial, and removal from office.

After more debate, the committee members voted one

by one—aye or nay. The article could pass with a simple majority of twenty votes, but Rodino hoped it wouldn't be that close. Television cameras focused on each tired face as the Democrats went first—twenty aye votes. Then the Republicans voted. Would there be bipartisan support? Eleven Republicans voted nay, six aye. As chairman, Rodino voted last. "Aye," he almost sighed. His voice was strained and hoarse. The ayes had it, 27-11, well more than a simple majority.

Peter Rodino had what he'd hoped for. No one could say the vote was nasty partisan politics. But he'd never wanted to impeach the president whose picture hung on his office wall. He went to the committee offices with several other representatives. The others talked quietly as Rodino leaned against his desk, exhausted. He crossed his arms over his chest and looked at the floor. Then his shoulders started to shake and tears ran down his face.[130]

Two days later, on Monday, July 29, the committee met again.

Article II, Abuse of Power.
    Using the powers of the office of President of the United States, Richard M. Nixon, in violation of his constitutional oath . . . has repeatedly

engaged in conduct violating the constitutional rights of citizens, impairing the due and proper administration of justice in the conduct of lawful inquiries, of contravening the law of governing agencies of the executive branch and the purposes of these agencies ...

Article II passed 28–10.

The last vote came on July 30.

Article III, Defiance of Subpoenas.

In his conduct of the office of President of the United States, Richard M. Nixon, contrary to his oath ... failed without lawful cause or excuse to produce papers and things as directed by duly authorized subpoenas issued by the Committee on the Judiciary of the House of Representatives on April 11, 1974, May 15, 1974, May 30, 1974, and June 24, 1974, and willfully disobeyed such subpoenas. ...

Article III passed 21–17.

Peter Rodino closed the committee's inquiry an hour before midnight on July 30. Now the matter would go before the entire House of Representatives—all 435 members. If a simple majority approved even one of the articles of impeachment, Richard Nixon would go to trial in the Senate.

Chairman Rodino had done his best and won high praise. But it wasn't over yet. If the full House voted to impeach, there was still the Senate trial. And if the Senate voted to convict, would Richard Nixon leave office peacefully? It was a frightening question.

CHAPTER 15

Reckoning
AUGUST 1974

F inally, Judge John Sirica had the tapes. At least some of them. Hours before the House Judiciary Committee finished its impeachment work on Tuesday, July 30, Richard Nixon turned over twenty subpoenaed tapes. The president's barricade was now hardly strong enough to stop a small breeze.

Six days later, on Monday, August 5, Nixon released three more tapes. They were tapes he had kept hidden not only from the special prosecutors, his staff, and the House Judiciary Committee, but also from his own lawyers. One was from June 23, 1972—six days after the Watergate break-in. During a long meeting, Nixon's chief of staff brought up several issues. At one point he said,

> Now, on the investigation ... the Democratic break-in thing, we're back in the problem area because the FBI is not under control ... they've been able to trace the money ... The way to handle this now is

for us to have [the CIA] call [the FBI] and just say, 'Stay . . . out of this—we don't want you to go any further.'

Nixon replied, "Right, fine." Then he suggested phony excuses the CIA could use to stop the FBI's investigation.[131]

That was it—the smoking gun, the ultimate witness.

The June 23 tape and the transcript of it that went to Congress and the public toppled what was left of the president's barricade. Richard Nixon did *not* learn about the cover-up in March 1973 as he had claimed for over a year. He had helped *start* the cover-up just days after the break-in. He'd been involved in obstruction of justice from the very beginning—keeping FBI investigators from getting to the truth and then bribing the accused burglars to keep them quiet. Moreover, he'd abused his presidential power by using a government agency, the CIA, for his own illegal purposes.

Members of the House Judiciary Committee who had wanted a smoking gun now had it (other tapes also showed strong evidence of criminal actions). The New Jersey Republican who'd stated so clearly that there was no direct evidence of Nixon's involvement in crimes said, "[The transcript] certainly changes my vote. This is devastating." Charles Wiggins, a Republican from California who'd defended the president throughout the investigation and debate, said with his voice breaking, "The magnificent career of Richard Nixon must be terminated . . ." He went back to his office and tore up the papers sitting on his desk. They were his notes for defending the president in the full House debate.[132]

By Wednesday, August 7, all the Republicans who had voted against the three articles of impeachment changed their minds. All voted aye, at least on the obstruction of justice charge.

In the Senate, which would act as the jury in an impeachment trial, Nixon's support collapsed as well. Senator Howard Baker had the answer to his question—what did the president know and when did he know it? On that same Wednesday, a group of Republican senators went to the White House and made it clear to the president that the full House *would* vote to impeach and the Senate *would* convict. Nixon would be removed from office—the Senate leaders had no doubt. Even the president's strongest defenders could no longer stand with him after the release of the June 23 tape. And if he stayed and faced trial, the senators told him, it would keep the nation in turmoil for weeks or even months.

Newspapers around the world announced Nixon's
resignation, August 9, 1974

The following evening, President Richard Nixon spoke
to the nation on television once more. Looking tired and
grim but in control, he announced that he would resign
the presidency the next day, August 9. No president had
ever resigned before. Nixon had put it off as long as he
could. As he always said, he wasn't a quitter. This was the
hardest thing he'd ever done.

At noon on Friday, August 9, Vice President Gerald
Ford took the presidential oath. Americans everywhere felt
a heavy weight lift off the country's shoulders. The United
States—the republic the Constitution established—had

been in grave danger. Its separation of powers and system of checks and balances had been threatened, its people's rights and protections violated, its democratic elections rigged. But in the end, Richard Nixon gave in to the system. He did not call on the military to defend him as some feared he would. He did not defy the Supreme Court. Instead, he left office before the full House of Representatives could vote to impeach and the Senate could vote to convict.

Former president Richard Nixon boarded a helicopter on the White House lawn as President Gerald Ford turned and walked into the White House to begin his presidency. Workers in government offices in Washington, DC, and around the country watched the peaceful transition of power on television and then got back to work. Military personnel did the same. So did American embassy staff in foreign countries. The United States had faced a constitutional crisis, and a president was forced to leave office mid-term for the first time in history. But the US government remained constant and stable. There was no coup, no revolt, no revolution, and no civil war. Dedicated government officials, a free press, and ordinary citizens had pushed the system of checks and balances to work, and the republic was safe.

. . .

Richard Nixon boards the presidential helicopter for the last time, August 9, 1974.

The trauma Watergate created still wasn't quite over. A month after taking office, President Gerald Ford used his constitutional power to grant Richard Nixon a full pardon. The grand jury would not be allowed to indict the disgraced former president as they'd wanted to. Nixon would not face a trial or prison time for anything connected to the Watergate scandal. He would not have to account for the abuses listed in the articles of impeachment. He would not have to defend himself against the 370 separate violations of law Republican Lowell Weicker listed in his report. Or explain how using taxpayers' money for a swimming pool, putting green, and pool table at his Florida home had anything to do with security. He would not need to apologize for the more than fifty secret and illegal investigations of American citizens he had instigated. The list could go on.

A majority of Americans thought Ford made a huge mistake with that pardon. After all, none of Nixon's aides or associates received pardons. Sixty-nine people faced charges for crimes related to Watergate. Forty-nine of those, including some forty government officials, were convicted.[133] The Nixon men who went to prison included John Dean, Bob Haldeman, John Ehrlichman, and John Mitchell, as well as James McCord, Howard Hunt, Gordon Liddy, and the other Watergate burglars. Over time, many of them talked or wrote about what they had done.

Several Nixon aides said that they slid into illegal activity one small step at a time. They didn't think of themselves as criminals even while they broke the law. They saw

President Gerald Ford answers questions from the House
Judiciary Committee about his decision to pardon Richard
Nixon, October 1974

their actions as protecting the president and his plans for
world peace and prosperity. The astonishing fact of having
a job in the White House and actually spending time in
the Oval Office went to their heads, many agreed. John
Dean saw it as a disease that he called "Ovalitis."

Worse, Nixon's aides put their loyalty to Richard Nixon
above the oath each had taken to uphold the Constitution.
Only when they left the White House did they realize the
seriousness of their actions.

Ford defended the pardon, saying he believed it was
best for the country to move forward. Seeing Richard

Nixon go through a criminal trial and perhaps go to prison would make the "long national nightmare" even worse. And it would weaken the United States in the eyes of the world. Historians still debate whether pardoning Nixon was the right thing to do.

Nixon returned home to his villa in San Clemente, California. He walked on the ocean beach and thought about ways to reconstruct his reputation. Even in disgrace, he wasn't a quitter and like most presidents, he worried about his place in history. He wrote his memoirs and books on foreign policy. He also gave interviews. In a lengthy television interview a few years after his resignation, Nixon said that he had made mistakes and let the nation and the American people down. But the former president never directly admitted that he had broken the law. Eventually, he regained *some* respect from *some* people for his foreign policy and environmental achievements as president. Richard Nixon died in 1994, twenty years after he left office, at the age of eighty-one.

Watergate is a half-century in the past, but its legacy continues. Americans in the twenty-first century don't trust their government or their president the way they did fifty years ago. In 1964, nearly 80 percent of Americans said they trusted the government to do what was right most of the time. Sixty-two percent of the nation still had

Former President Nixon and his wife, Pat, at their home in San Clemente, California

strong confidence in government when Nixon started his first term. By the time Richard Nixon left office in 1974, however, that number had dropped to 36 percent.[134]

Watergate wasn't the only reason for the slide in confidence. The war in Vietnam played a big part. And so did the Pentagon Papers by showing that presidents and other officials had lied to the American people. Difficult race relations and a struggling economy damaged people's confidence in government as well. But the awful details of Richard Nixon's abuse of power and obstruction of justice had a huge impact on people's loss of trust. Americans felt betrayed and wronged, with good reason.

The result, though, was that many people now hesitated to trust anything any government official told them. And they passed that mistrust on to the next generation. Confidence in government has never again reached the levels of the 1960s no matter who is in office.[135]

Complete lack of trust in government is dangerous. For example, government workers give Americans information on everything from bacteria on lettuce to the need for seat belts and the threat of identity theft. When people don't trust the government at all, they can put themselves or their families at risk from wildfires, hurricanes, serious illnesses, epidemics, and more.

But while that kind of mistrust is dangerous, Watergate taught many Americans that *unquestioning* trust is just as bad. Unfortunately, Richard Nixon wasn't the first or last president to lie. By 1974, many Americans realized that they *needed* to ask questions and demand solid, provable information from candidates and government officials. They needed to keep up with the news and figure out which news sources to trust. For all of Nixon's raging against the press, most Americans gradually gained new respect for investigative reporting in newspapers and other news outlets. And as one Watergate news story after another was proven to be accurately reported and true, a number of people even viewed journalists like Woodward and Bernstein as heroes.

· · ·

Three months after Nixon resigned, Americans voted in Congressional and state elections. Their disgust with all that happened resulted in big gains for Democrats in the House of Representatives, the Senate, and in several states. Many people supported candidates who pledged to reform and strengthen laws that would open windows on political and government activity. They hoped this transparency would prevent another Watergate.

The new Congress passed laws regulating campaign donations to avoid the kind of corruption that spread through Nixon's 1972 campaign. In particular, those laws limited the amount of money that businesses and corporations could give a candidate. Congress also established the Federal Election Commission to oversee campaigns and be sure they followed the laws.

A new Privacy Act limited the ways government could use people's personal information such as tax returns or phone records. And Congress restricted the CIA and other intelligence agencies' power to spy on United States citizens.

Reforms to existing laws made it harder for the president or other government officials to keep information from Congress or the public. Now only the appropriate authorities could label information classified (secret).

And only if it met strict new rules. Another new law made all White House and presidential records the property of the American people. When the president leaves office, his or her records go to the National Archives and may not be destroyed. Ethics laws set behavior guidelines for elected and appointed officials as well. And presidents after Nixon started setting clear rules that give the Department of Justice and the FBI independence in some kinds of law enforcement investigations. The list of reforms goes on.

What about today?
Are those reform laws still in effect?

Some are. Some are not.

Legislatures change laws as times change. In the decades after Watergate, Congress revised many of the laws passed following the scandal. After the terrorist attacks of September 11, 2001, fear of more attacks led Congress to write a law loosening rules for American intelligence agencies. The new law made it easier for these agencies to keep track of the phones, e-mails, and bank records of American citizens. Intelligence officials argued that new technology allowed terrorists and criminals to communicate and plan in ways that didn't exist in the 1970s. They said the new law simply expanded the use of tactics that law enforcement was already using against organized crime. Critics argued that the new law allowed for unacceptable violations of the Fourth Amendment and chipped away at Americans' freedoms. Congress has revised the 2001 law more than once, but it is still controversial.

Campaign finance laws have changed several times since Watergate too. In 2010, a divided Supreme Court ruled 5–4 that corporations can spend unlimited amounts of money on political advertising. They ruled that this was part of a corporation's right to free speech. The decision did away with parts of earlier campaign laws and overturned two previous Supreme Court decisions. Critics argue that corporations are not people and don't have the same constitutional rights people do. They say that the 2010 decision allows unlimited election spending. Groups or businesses that want to eliminate safety rules or environmental protections can use their financial power to get what they want. Critics also say that the decision allows corporate money to influence elections, policies, and laws in ways that individual citizens cannot. Other reforms, including changes in government spending rules, a new government ethics office, and more, are still in effect today.

While the practice of giving law enforcement agencies independence from the Oval Office is not law, it remained the policy of every president between 1974 and 2017. However, presidents don't have to follow such a policy, and President Donald Trump generally chose not to.

Attitudes toward the news media have changed since Watergate too. At that time, the White House convinced many people that they could not trust major newspapers, but the facts proved that that wasn't the case. Today, however, some politicians and cable newscasters have led many Americans to again believe that they cannot trust mainstream newspapers and television network news outlets. Yet there is almost no evidence to support their accusations that the mainstream media lies or reports false or fake news.

Could something like Watergate happen again? Sadly, the answer is yes—it could happen and it has happened in some cases despite efforts to prevent it. People, including political leaders, aren't perfect. And the power that leaders have often pushes them to want even more power.

. . .

The question isn't whether a president will violate his or her oath or try to destroy the system of checks and balances. The question is whether Americans in the legislative, executive, and judicial branches of government—as well as the press and the public—will step forward to stop an abuse of power. Whether they will act to preserve their republic.

Both Democrats and Republicans on the Senate and House committees in 1973 and 1974 took risks. They risked losing their party's and the president's support and angering the people who elected them. It wasn't easy, but in the end they put the country before their political parties or personal gain.

Brave men and women who worked for government agencies during the Watergate scandal took risks too. They refused to follow orders when obeying them would have violated their oath to uphold the Constitution. Two attorneys general and two special prosecutors and their staffs did the same thing.

Judge John Sirica and the members of the Supreme Court set aside their political leanings in 1974. They based their decisions on the law and the Constitution. That's what judges and justices are supposed to do.

And what about the press? The news media has

changed a lot since the 1970s. But its role remains the same, or should. In 2012, Bob Woodward and Carl Bernstein got together again and wrote an article for a conference. They said about Watergate, "editors gave us the time and encouragement to pursue an intricate, elusive story . . . and then the rest of the American system (Congress, the judiciary) took over and worked."[136] That's why the founders of the United States protected a free press—so it could push and inform the system.

Finally, there's the public—We the People of the United States. Will Americans take their responsibilities seriously? Will they look for the truth in what they read and hear and see? Citizens have a duty to be informed. They need to recognize the warning signs of misinformation—scare tactics, accusations without evidence, claims that journalists are the enemy, vague promises. It takes effort to sort through twenty-first-century news sources—social media, cable and satellite news outlets, mainstream media, etc. But it's the only way to find the real facts. And when there is solid evidence of wrongdoing in government, Americans have to demand action.

And what about the power of the vote? Will Americans elect candidates who are strong enough to do what's right? Will they stand against candidates who promote hate or who lie about their opponents or themselves?

President Lyndon Johnson said, the "vote is the most powerful instrument ever devised by man for breaking down injustice. . . ." Voting is a serious responsibility and an important part of protecting and preserving the American republic.

That's the real lesson of Watergate. The framers designed a remarkable Constitution with built-in safeguards against any one person's abuse of power. But that Constitution is just words on a page if individual Americans don't make it work in the real world.

We the People. The American people, all of them, are the engine that makes the system work.

Bibliography

Archer, Jules. *Watergate: A Story of Richard Nixon and the Shocking 1972 Scandal.* New York: Sky Pony Press, 1975.

Bernstein, Carl, and Bob Woodward. *All the President's Men.* New York: Simon & Schuster, 1974

Bernstein, Carl, and Bob Woodward. "FBI Finds Nixon Aides Sabotaged Democrats." *Washington Post*, October 10, 1972. https://search.proquest.com/hnpwashingtonpost/docview/148302252/743028F5457945CEPQ

Bernstein, Carl, and Bob Woodward. "GOP Hits *Post* for Hearsay." *Washington Post*, October 17, 1972. https://search.proquest.com/hnpwashingtonpost/docview/148186757/A965487A35A34A9CPQ

Bernstein, Carl, and Bob Woodward. "Hunt Urges 4 to Admit Guilt." *Washington Post*, January 15, 1973. https://search.proquest.com/hnpwashingtonpost/docview/148478798/F92DAE0881A74BCDPQ

Bernstein, Carl, and Bob Woodward. "Still Secret: Who Hired Spies and Why." *Washington Post*, January 31, 1973. https://search.proquest.com/hnpwashingtonpost/docview/148518019/A0BFF9B788214B18PQ/14

"Beyond Distrust: How Americans View Their Government." Pew Research Center, US Politics and Policy, November 23, 2015. https://www.people-press.org/2015/11/23/1-trust-in-government-1958-2015/

Campbell, W. Joseph. "Five Media Myths of Watergate." BBC News. June 17, 2012. https://www.bbc.com/news/magazine-18215048

Cooke, Alistair. "Senator Sam Ervin." *Letter from America.* April 28, 1985. https://www.bbc.co.uk/programmes/b043xkql

Dash, Samuel. *Chief Counsel: Inside the Ervin Committee—the Untold Story of Watergate*. New York: Random House, 1976.

Dean, John W. *The Nixon Defense: What He Knew and When He Knew It*. New York: Viking, 2014.

Doyle, James. *Not Above the Law: The Battles of Watergate Prosecutors Cox and Jaworski*. New York: William Morrow and Company, Inc. 1977.

Drew, Elizabeth. *Washington Journal: Reporting Watergate and Richard Nixon's Downfall*. New York: Overlook Duckworth, 2015.

Emery, Fred. *Watergate: The Corruption of American Politics and the Fall of Richard Nixon*. New York: Times Books, 1994.

Ervin, Sam J., Jr. *The Whole Truth: The Watergate Conspiracy*. New York: Random House, 1980.

"Gallup Presidential Election Trial-Heat Trends, 1936–2008." Gallup. https://news.gallup.com/poll/110548/gallup-presidential-election-trial-heat-trends.aspx

Gerstenzang, James. "Sen. Howard Baker dies at 88; majority leader and Reagan's chief of staff." *Washington Post*, June 26, 2014. https://www.washingtonpost.com/national/sen-howard-baker-majority-leader-and-reagans-chief-of-staff-dies-at-88/2014/06/26/2e84ff30-c5da-11df-94e1-c5afa35a9e59_story.html

Graham, Katharine. *Personal History*. New York: Vintage Books, 1997.

Greider, William. "Wonders of Watergate: Nixon Tapes Provide Ultimate Witness." *Washington Post*, July 17, 1973. https://search.proquest.com/hnpwashingtonpost/docview/148411918/F85C-74C1697940E9PQ

Herbers, John. "Nixon's Presidency: Centralized Control." *New York Times*, March 6, 1973. https://www.nytimes.com/1973/03/06/archives/nixons-presidency-centralized-control-nixons-presidency-an-attempt.html

Hersh, Seymour. "4 Watergate Defendants Reported Still Being Paid." *New York Times*, January 14, 1973. https://www.nytimes.com/1973/01/14/archives/4-watergate-defendants-reported-still-being-paid-major-points.html

Hodgson, Godfrey. "Samuel Dash." *The Guardian*, June 10, 2004.https://www.theguardian.com/news/2004/jun/11/guardianobituaries.usa

Jaworski, Leon. *The Right and the Power: The Prosecution of Watergate.* New York: Pocket Books, 1977.

Jefferson, Thomas. Thomas Jefferson to Charles Yancey, letter, January 6, 1816, Jefferson Papers, National Archives.

Jefferson, Thomas. Thomas Jefferson to James Currie, letter, January 28, 1786, Jefferson Papers, National Archives.

Johnson, Lyndon B. "Remarks on the Signing of the Voting Rights Act," August 6, 1965. https://millercenter.org/the-presidency/presidentialspeeches/august-6-1965-remarks-signing-voting-rights-act.

Lee, Mordecai. *Nixon's Super-Secretaries: The Last Grand Presidential Reorganization Effort.* College Station, TX: Texas A&M University Press, 2010.

Lewis, Alfred E. "5 Held in Plot to Bug Democrats' Office Here." *Washington Post*, June 18, 1972. https://search.proquest.com/hn-pwashingtonpost/docview/148299270/EAF56A54B0F94961PQ

Lewis, Anthony. "United States v. Nixon." *New York Times*, July 25, 1974. https://www.nytimes.com/1974/07/25/archives/united-states-v-nixon-abroad-at-home.html

Linder, Douglas O. "Case Dismissed: Judge Matthew Byrne's Ruling in the Trial of Daniel Ellsberg and Anthony Russo (May 11, 1973)." Famous Trials. https://famous-trials.com/ellsberg/276-rule

Madison, James, Hamilton, Alexander and J. Jay. *The Federalist Papers.* London: Penguin Books, 1987 (1787).

Magruder, Jeb Stuart. *An American Life: One Man's Road to Watergate*. New York: Atheneum, 1974.

Manas, Steve. "Peter Rodino: Alumnus Championed the Constitution." *Rutgers Today*, October 10, 2016. https://news.rutgers.edu/feature/peter-rodino-alumnus-championed-constitution/20160926#.Xi4AESN7k2w

Murray, Patrick. "Public Opinion on Impeachment: Lessons from Watergate." Monmouth University Polling Institute, June 12, 2017.

Neyfakh, Leon. "Saturday Night." (Includes interview with Jim Doyle and Carl Feldbaum), in *Slow Burn*: Season 1, Episode 7, podcast audio, January 17, 2018.

Neyfakh, Leon. "Lie Detectors." (Includes interview with Mary Diorio) in Slow Burn: Season 1, Episode 4, podcast audio, December 19, 2017.

Nixon, Richard. "First Watergate Speech", April 30, 1973. https://watergate.info/1973/04/30/nixons-first-watergate-speech.html

Nixon, Richard M. press conference, November 17, 1973.

Perlstein, Rick. *Nixonland: The Rise of a President and the Fracturing of America*. New York: Scribner, 2008.

Policinski, Gene. "Watergate Era: 'A' Peak in Journalism." Freedom Forum Institute, May 9, 2013. https://www.freedomforuminstitute.org/2013/05/09/watergate-era-a-peak-in-journalism/

Roosevelt, Franklin. "On the Recession." Radio address, April 14, 1938. https://millercenter.org/the-presidency/presidential-speeches/april-14-1938-fireside-chat-12-recession

Sirica, John J. *To Set the Record Straight: The Break-in, The Tapes, The Conspirators, The Pardon*. New York: W. W. Norton & Company, 1979.

Taylor, Jessica. "Fractured into Factions? What the Founders Feared about Impeachment." *Trump Impeachment Iquiry*, NPR, November 18, 2019. https://www.npr.org/2019/11/18/779938819/fractured-into-factions-what-the-founders-feared-about-impeachment

"The Fateful Vote to Impeach." *Time*. August 5, 1974. https://time.com/3079519/the-fateful-vote-to-impeach/

"The *Washington Post*'s Cameron Barr joins Oxford Union for a debate on the media." WashPost PR Blog, November 21, 2019. https://www.washingtonpost.com/pr/2019/11/21/washington-posts-cameron-barr-joins-oxford-union-debate-media/

Thomas, Evan. *Being Nixon: A Man Divided*. New York: Random House, 2015.

"Watergate Casualties and Convictions." Watergate.info. https://watergate.info/analysis/casualties-and-convictions

Watergate Plus 30: Shadow of History. PBS Home Video, 2003.

Weiner, Tim. *One Man Against the World: The Tragedy of Richard Nixon*. New York: Henry Holt and Company, 2015.

White, Theodore H. *Breach of Faith: The Fall of Richard Nixon*. New York: Atheneum, 1975.

Woodward, Bob. *The Last of the President's Men*. New York: Simon & Schuster, 2015.

Woodward, Bob. *The Secret Man: The Story of Watergate's Deep Throat*. New York: Simon & Schuster, 2005.

Woodward, Bob, and Carl Bernstein. *The Final Days: The Classic, Behind-the-Scenes Account of Richard Nixon's Dramatic Last Days in the White House*. New York: Simon & Schuster Paperbacks, 1976.

Watergate Timeline

Key

> **Italics indicate an event that was not known to the public or the press until later**

1968

November

Richard Nixon is elected president in a very close race

1969

January

Richard Nixon inaugurated as the thirty-seventh president of the United States

October

Hundreds of thousands march for an end to the war in Vietnam; though half of all Americans still support the war.

1970

July

Nixon approves a secret plan for using the FBI, CIA, and other agencies for intelligence-gathering on US citizens (he changed his mind but came back to the plan later)

1971

June

The *New York Times* begins publishing the Pentagon Papers—a secret Defense Department history of the Vietnam War; the *Washington Post* begins publishing the papers days later

The Nixon administration asks the federal courts to force the newspapers to stop publishing the Pentagon Papers

The Supreme Court rules in favor of the *New York Times* and the *Washington Post*

July

White House aides suggest to the president creating a secret security group to operate outside authorized security agencies; the group is known as "the Plumbers"

September

The Plumbers burglarize the office of Daniel Ellsberg's doctor to find files that might damage Ellsberg's defense in his espionage trial and promote negative public opinion toward him

1972

February–March

Senator Edmund Muskie's campaign for the Democratic nomination falters; *he and other Democrats are victims of the Nixon campaign's "dirty tricks" operations*

Nixon visits communist China and later, the Soviet Union; the first American president to visit communist countries

June

Five men are arrested during a break-in at the Democratic National Headquarters in the Watergate complex

James McCord, a former CIA employee and head of security for the Committee to Reelect the President (CRP), is one of the burglars arrested; police discover a White House phone number

Bob Woodward and Carl Bernstein of the *Washington Post* report on the break-in, and editors assign them to the story full-time

John Mitchell, former attorney general and head of the Nixon campaign, denies any link between the burglary and the president or his campaign

Nixon discusses the break-in with Chief of Staff Bob Haldeman; Nixon decides to limit the FBI's investigation of the burglary and will use the CIA to do this

August

Woodward and Bernstein report that a $25,000 donation to the Nixon reelection campaign was deposited in the bank account of one of the Watergate burglars

September

A grand jury indicts the five men arrested at the Watergate offices, as well as two men who oversaw the burglary; Judge John Sirica schedules their trial for after the November election

Woodward and Bernstein report that while attorney general, John Mitchell controlled a secret fund used to finance intelligence-gathering against Democrats

October

FBI agents say that the Watergate break-in was part of a "massive campaign of political spying and sabotage" by the Nixon campaign

November

Nixon is elected for a second term in one of the largest land-slides in American history

1973

January

Judge John Sirica presides over the trial of the Watergate burglars and handlers; five plead guilty; the trial jury finds the other two guilty on all charges

Richard Nixon is inaugurated for his second term

February

The Senate votes to create a Senate Select Committee to investigate Watergate

March

Convicted burglar James McCord admits in a letter to Judge Sirica that he and the other burglars lied under White House pressure and that there are other men involved in the Watergate burglary and cover-up

April

White House Counsel John Dean agrees to cooperate with federal prosecutors

The *New York Daily News* and the *Washington Post* report that the acting director of the FBI destroyed evidence related to Watergate; the director resigns

Nixon announces that his top aides, Haldeman and Ehrlichman, and the attorney general have resigned; he has fired White House Counsel John Dean

May

The judge in the Daniel Ellsberg trial dismisses all charges against Ellsberg after learning of government misconduct in the case and of the burglary of Ellsberg's doctor's office by the same men who broke into the Watergate offices

The Senate Watergate Committee begins its nationally televised hearings

Archibald Cox is appointed Watergate special prosecutor to look into possible misdeeds by the White House

June

The *Washington Post* reports that John Dean has told investigators that he discussed the Watergate cover-up with the president at least thirty-five times

John Dean begins testifying before the Senate Watergate Committee by reading a 245-page account of the Watergate cover-up

July

Former White House aide Alexander Butterfield tells Senate committee that all conversations in the Oval Office were recorded at the order of the president

The Senate committee and the special prosecutor request several tape recordings from the president; the president refuses

The Senate Committee and the special prosecutor issue subpoenas for the tapes; Nixon refuses, claiming executive privilege

October

Vice President Spiro Agnew resigns after evidence that he accepted bribes emerges

Gerald Ford is sworn in as vice president

Nixon fires Attorney General Elliot Richardson and his deputy because they refuse to fire Special Prosecutor Archibald Cox; Nixon orders the next in command at the Justice Department to fire Cox; an enormous negative public response follows

Nixon bows to pressure, releases some tapes, and appoints a new special prosecutor

November

Leon Jaworski becomes the new Watergate special prosecutor

White House lawyers announce that two subpoenaed tapes are missing; a third tape has an eighteen-and-a-half-minute gap

1974

February

The House of Representatives votes to have the House Judiciary Committee investigate possible grounds for impeachment of the president; Peter Rodino chairs the committee

The Watergate grand jury indicts seven former White House aides; *the grand jury also names Richard Nixon as an unindicted coconspirator*

March

Judge Sirica sends the grand jury's sealed report to the House Judiciary Committee

April

Special Prosecutor Leon Jaworski subpoenas sixty-four White House tapes

Refusing to turn over the subpoenaed tapes, the president releases edited transcripts of some tapes to the House Judiciary Committee; the public is shocked by the conversations and language in the transcripts

May

The House Judiciary Committee begins closed impeachment hearings

The Supreme Court agrees to hear arguments on the issue of the tapes

July

The Supreme Court hears arguments in *United States v. Richard M. Nixon*

The Supreme Court rules unanimously that the president does have the right to claim executive privilege but not in all cases and not in this case; the president is ordered to turn over the White House tapes

The House Judiciary Committee adopts three articles of impeachment against the president, all with bipartisan support; the articles will go to the full House of Representatives for a vote

August

Nixon releases transcripts of three more tapes. the tape reveals that the president knew about and participated in a cover-up of the crimes associated with the Watergate break-in within days of the burglary

All eleven Republican members of the House Judiciary Committee now say they will change their votes and support impeachment

President Richard Nixon resigns from office; Gerald Ford becomes president

Cast of Characters—by category

White House/CRP

Richard Nixon—thirty-seventh president of the United States, January 1969–August 1974; first president to resign

James McCord—security coordinator for the Committee to Reelect the President and one of the Watergate burglars

John Mitchell—attorney general of the United States, later chairman of the Committee to Reelect the President

E. Howard Hunt—consultant to the White House, part of the break-ins at the Watergate complex and the office of Daniel Ellsberg's doctor

Hugh Sloan—treasurer of the Committee to Reelect the President; resigned shortly after the Watergate break-in

Bob Haldeman—White House chief of staff

G. Gordon Liddy—White House staff assistant, counsel to the Committee to Reelect the President, part of the break-ins at the Watergate complex and the office of Daniel Ellsberg's doctor

John Dean—counsel to the president and key witness in Senate Watergate hearings

John Ehrlichman—assistant to the president

Alexander Butterfield—deputy assistant to the president

Elliot Richardson—attorney general of the United States

Spiro Agnew—vice president of the United States, January 1969–October 1973

William Ruckelshaus—deputy attorney general of the United States

Gerald Ford—first appointed (not elected) vice president of the United States; thirty-eighth president of the United States, August 1974–January 1977

Alexander Haig—White House chief of staff

Press

Bob Woodward—investigative reporter for the *Washington Post*

Carl Bernstein—investigative reporter for the *Washington Post*

Katharine Graham—the first twentieth-century woman to serve as publisher of a major newspaper in the US; owner and publisher of the *Washington Post*

Ben Bradlee—executive editor of the *Washington Post*

Historical

James Madison—"Father of the Constitution" and coauthor of the Federalist Papers, US secretary of state, US vice president, fourth president of the United States, 1809–1817

George Washington—"Father of the Country," commander of the Continental Army during the American Revolution, president of the Constitutional Convention, first president of the United States, 1789–1797

Roger Sherman—Connecticut delegate to the Constitutional Convention

James Wilson—Pennsylvania delegate to the Constitutional Convention

Thomas Jefferson—author of the Declaration of Independence, third president of the United States, 1801–1809

Andrew Johnson—seventeenth president of the United States and first president to be impeached

Adolf Hitler—leader of the Nazi Party of Germany, ruled Germany as a dictator, 1933–1945; responsible for the Holocaust and World War II

Edmund Burke—eighteenth-century Anglo-Irish statesman and philosopher

Alexander Hamilton—New York delegate to the Constitutional Convention, coauthor of the Federalist Papers, first secretary of the treasury

John Marshall—chief justice of the United States, 1801–1835

Special Prosecutor's Office

Archibald Cox—special prosecutor, May–October 1973

Carl Feldbaum—attorney for the Office of the Special Prosecutor

Phil Bakes—counsel to the special prosecutor

Leon Jaworski—special prosecutor, November 1973–October 1974

Philip Lacovara—counsel to the special prosecutor

US Senate

Sam Dash—chief counsel to the Senate Watergate Committee

Sam Ervin—US senator from North Carolina and chair of the Senate Watergate Committee

Howard Baker—US senator from Tennessee and member of the Senate Watergate Committee

Lowell Weicker—US senator from Connecticut and member of the Senate Watergate Committee

US House of Representatives

Peter Rodino—US representative from New Jersey and chair of the House Judiciary Committee

John Doar—chief counsel to the House Judiciary Committee

Hamilton Fish—US representative from New York and member of the House Judiciary Committee

Thomas Railsback—US representative from Illinois and member of the House Judiciary Committee

Walter Flowers—US representative from Alabama and member of the House Judiciary Committee

M. Caldwell Butler—US representative from Virginia and member of the House Judiciary Committee

Barbara Jordan—US representative from Texas and member of the House Judiciary Committee

Charles Wiggins—US representative from California and member of the House Judiciary Committee

Judiciary

John Sirica—chief judge, US District Court for the District of Columbia

Judges US Court of Appeals for the District of Columbia Circuits

United States Supreme Court Justices

Other

George McGovern—US senator from South Dakota and Democratic nominee for president in 1972

Edmund Muskie—US senator from Maine and early frontrunner in race for Democratic presidential nomination, 1972

Daniel Ellsberg—military analyst responsible for leaking the Pentagon Papers to major newspapers

Angelo Lano—FBI agent

Endnotes

1 Weiner, *One Man Against the World*, 218.

2 Emery, *Watergate*, 223.

3 Ibid., 224.

4 Weiner, 209.

5 White, *Breach of Faith*, 198–199.

6 Weiner, 133.

7 Ibid., 123.

8 Emery, 180.

9 Bernstein and Woodward, *All the President's Men*, 13–14.

10 Ibid., 18–19.

11 Ibid., 19.

12 *Washington Post*, "5 Held in Plot to Bug Democrats' Office Here."

13 Bernstein and Woodward, 19–20.

14 Ibid., 15, 20.

15 "Gallup Presidential Election Trial-Heat Trends, 1936–2008."

16 Bernstein and Woodward, 20–22.

17 Jefferson, letter to James Currie, January 28, 1786.

18 Jefferson, letter to Charles Yancey, January 6, 1816.

19 Bernstein and Woodward, 24.

20 Ibid., 25.

21 Ibid., 44.

22 Ibid., 59.

23 Ibid., 59–60.

24 Ibid., 61.

25 Ibid., 61–62.

26 Ibid.

27 Woodward, *The Secret Man*, 65–66.

28 Bernstein and Woodward, 64.

29 Ibid., 57.

30 Ibid., 97.

31 Ibid., 105.

32 *Washington Post*, "FBI Finds Nixon Aides Sabotaged Democrats."

33 *Washington Post*, "GOP Hits *Post* for Hearsay."

34 Bernstein and Woodward, 166.

35 BBC News online, "Five Media Myths of Watergate."

36 Graham, *Personal History*, 476.

37 Bernstein and Woodward, 220.

38 Graham, 481-482.

39 Emery, 238.

40 *New York Times*, "4 Watergate Defendants Reported Still Being Paid."

41 *Washington Post*, "Hunt Urges 4 to Admit Guilt."

42 Emery, 239.

43 *Washington Post*, "Still Secret."

44 Doyle, *Not Above the Law*, 32.

45 Emery, 240.

46 Dash, Chief Counsel, 29.

47 Ibid., 30.

48 Ibid.

49 Ibid., 74.

50 Ibid., 21.

51 Ibid., 61.

52 Ibid., 85–86.

53 Bernstein and Woodward, 306.

54 Famous Trials online, "Case Dismissed."

55 Dash, 84.

56 Ibid., 85.

57 Ibid., 109–110.

58 Ibid., 116.

59 *Watergate Plus 30.*

60 Dash, 161.

61 Ibid., 164.

62 Ibid., 166.

63 *Washington Post*, "Sen. Howard Baker dies at 88."

64 Dash, 179–180.

65 *Washington Post*, "Wonders of Watergate."

66 Cooke, "Senator Sam Ervin."

67 Ervin, *The Whole Truth*, 189.

68 *Washington Post* PR Blog, "The *Washington Post*'s Cameron Barr joins Oxford Union for a debate on the media."

69 Doyle, 42.

70 Emery, 357.

71 Doyle, 37.

72 Ibid, 60–61.

73 Ibid., 92–93.

74 Dash, 175.

75 Ibid., 197.

76 Ibid., 67.

77 Ibid.

78 Ervin, 35.

79 Sirica, *To Set the Record Straight*, 140.

80 Ibid., 159.

81 Emery, 378.

82 Ibid., 385.

83 Drew, *Wasington Journal*, 31.

84 Doyle, 131.

85 Drew, 40.

86 Ibid., 49.

87 Emery, 395.

88 Doyle, 185.

89 *Slow Burn*, "Saturday Night."

90 Doyle, 195.

91 Doyle, 201.

92 Drew, 164.

93 Franklin Roosevelt, "On the Recession." April 14, 1938.

94 Doyle, 204.

95 Ibid., 207.

96 Ibid., 209.

97 Ibid., 200.

98 White, 344.

99 Monmouth University Polling Institute online, "Public Opinion on Impeachment."

100 Emery, 402.

101 Ibid., 405.

102 Doyle, 205.

103 Archer, *Watergate*, 238.

104 White, 361.

105 Emery, 420.

106 Ibid.

107 *Rutgers Today* online, "Peter Rodino."

108 Archer, 252.

109 Ibid., 250.

110 *Slow Burn*

111 Drew, 304.

112 Ibid.

113 Ibid., 91.

114 Doyle, 241.

115 Drew, 306.

116 *New York Times*, "United States v. Nixon."

117 Drew, 333.

118 Doyle, 338.

119 Ibid., 340.

120 Drew, 300.

121 NPR, "Fractured into Factions?"

122 Drew, 322.

123 Ibid., 334.

124 Ibid., 323.

125 Emery, 444.

126 *Time*, "The Fateful Vote to Impeach."

127 Drew, 337–350.

128 *Time*, "The Fateful Vote to Impeach."

129 Drew, 349–350.

130 *Rutgers Today* online, "Peter Rodino."

131 Drew, 391.

132 Ibid., 404–405.

133 Watergate.info, "Watergate Casualties and Convictions."

134 Pew Research Center online, "Beyond Distrust."

135 Pew Research Center online, "Ibid."

136 Freedom Forum Institute online, "Watergate Era: 'A' Peak in Journalism."

Index

31901067275190